CW01512887

Forensic Science Basics

Every Contact Leaves a Trace

by David Holding

First published by
Scott Martin Productions, 2020
www.scottmartinproductions.com

First published in Great Britain in 2020 by
Scott Martin Productions
10 Chester Place,
Adlington, Chorley, PR6 9RP
scottmartinproductions@gmail.com
www.scottmartinproductions.com

Electronic version and paperback versions available
for purchase on Amazon.
Copyright (c) David Holding and Scott Martin
Productions.

First edition 2020.

Acknowledgements

I am most grateful for the encouragement and support I have received from many quarters in the preparation of this work. In particular, I wish to express my thanks to members of the medical, legal and forensic professions, for sharing with me their expertise and opinions on the matters covered. My appreciation also extends to members of the Department of Forensic Science at the University of Central Lancashire, and the ever-helpful staff at the various libraries and archives I have consulted during my research. My gratitude loses no sincerity in its generality.

Last, but by no means least, my sincere thanks must go to my publisher, Lesley Atherton, whose unfailing support has never failed. This support has provided the impetus to complete this work during a period of uncertainty and apprehension. It is my hope that this work will provide a welcome distraction for readers, and stimulate in them an interest in a subject that has fascinated me from my student days and continues to do so.

David Holding 2020

Contents

Also by David Holding:

Murder in the Heather: The Winter Hill Murder of 1838.

The Pendle Witch Trials of 1612.

The Dark Figure: Crime in Victorian Bolton.

Bleak Christmas: The Pretoria Colliery Disaster of 1910.

Doctors in the Dock: The Trials of Doctors Harold Shipman, John Bodkin Adams and Buck Ruxton.

Introduction

The word 'science' derives from the Latin *scientia,* which is itself derived from the verb *sciri* meaning 'to know'. So science is about 'knowledge'.

The word 'forensic' is also Latin in origin and derives from the word *forensis,* which means 'in open court'. From 'forensis' comes the word 'forum' - a public square found in the centre of most Roman towns, where matters were argued and adjudicated.

The modern usage of the word 'forensic' refers to a 'form of legal evidence'. However, a more useful working definition is that 'forensic science' is a science used to assist the legal process in the investigation of crime by providing evidence.

Forensic science has a tripartite structure consisting of 'collection' which refers to scientific investigation, 'examination' which is concerned with scientific analysis of evidence, and finally, 'presentation' which pertains to criminal trials. A forensic case will involve all aspects of each of the three structured elements, each being equally important. Each step in forensic science must be taken in an exact sequence to ensure that the investigation is in no doubt about what is being debated.

We can define the purpose of 'forensic' science as being to provide objective information on which reliable, evidence-based decisions can be made. Forensic science deals with 'real or physical' evidence. In other words, evidence based on the discovery and examination of 'material' sources. This is in contrast with 'testimonial' or documentary evidence which are verbal or written accounts of a particular event. However, if we accept that 'real' evidence is more reliable than testimonial evidence, this does not necessarily imply that it is absolute or infallible.

Contrary to popular perception, science is a highly uncertain area of knowledge. It does not deal in certainties but 'probabilities'. So when interpreting a crime scene or evidence taken for analysis, the forensic scientist is not looking for what happened, but what 'probably' happened. Eventually, a report is produced that presents the results of the analysis in terms of 'probability' not certainty.

However, 'real' evidence is a valuable property in that it opens up a huge range of potential additional evidence that is mostly unseen or unrecognised by the layperson. In the words of Dr Paul Kirk (in 1974 while the head of the criminology faculty at the University of Berkeley in the United States): "*Whatever the criminal leaves, even unconsciously, will serve as a silent witness against him*". In effect, Kirk was restating a concept which has become enshrined in traditional forensic investigation, namely the *Locard Exchange Principle*.

This principle is usually summarised as 'every contact leaves a trace'. The concept proposed here is that contact between people and objects or other people will inevitably involve the transfer of such traces as hair, fibres and DNA. It is these traces which provide evidence to link an offender to a crime scene or victim. Forensic evidence begins at the crime scene where there is the need to identify and recover the material objects that will form the basis of the 'real' evidence. Procedures at the crime scene are designed to control, preserve, record and recover evidence that will allow investigators to reconstruct the events that occurred at the scene.

Crime scenes in popular TV crime dramas are usually examined and quickly concluded by one of the principal characters in the drama with minimal assistance from others. Often termed as the "CSI Effect," these programmes give the public a false impression of investigations. In reality, the crime scene examination at major crimes is essentially a 'team' effort, involving many people, each with their own specific role to play.

The usual personnel in attendance at a crime scene will include a Crime Scene Manager (CSM), who has overall responsibility for coordinating the examination of the scene, the Scenes of Crime Officer (SOCO) who will search the scene, and an Investigating Officer from the police.

Depending on the circumstances of the crime and the extent of the search for evidence, some crime scenes require the presence of more specialist investigators.

These can include a forensic pathologist whose role is to examine the body at the scene followed by a post-mortem examination.

A forensic anthropologist may be required to examine human skeletal remains, and an entomologist to interpret insect activity on the body and to estimate the time of death of the victim.

Any one of the many people involved in crime scene investigation has a clear duty not only to record the obvious signs at the scene but also to examine and observe what the evidence reveals to them. It is also essential that they must be prepared and welcome the opportunity to combine their knowledge and expertise with the skills of other professionals, to adopt a holistic approach to every investigation.

If the crime scene is where the contribution of forensic science begins, then the starting point will be the initial reporting of an incident to the police. The crucial first step is an examination of the scene by the police officers who responded to the notification of an incident. It is they that have to evaluate the scene and determine whether or not a crime has in fact been committed. A decision also has to be made regarding what level of response is required. For serious crimes, this will inevitably involve informing senior detectives and scene investigators.

The following chapters in this work are organised into selected topics covering crime scene investigation, individual identification, time of death, causes of death and much more. Each of the chapters begins with an informative discussion of the various elements of specific investigative techniques involved in the analysis of evidence. Modern forensic laboratories use a vast range of scientific specialities to exonerate the innocent and help convict the guilty. It is these combined specialities which constitute 'forensic' science and which this work describes in detail.

A useful strategy for investigating crime and its implementation could involve finding factual answers to the following six pertinent questions:

What happened?
Who was involved?
Where did it happen?
When did it happen?
How did it happen?
Why did it happen?

The importance of these six questions to the investigation of crime is that reconstruction of a crime scene must not use them to find evidence that supports <u>preconceived</u> ideas. Instead, investigators must seek answers to each of these questions as the investigation progresses and only then evaluate them as a whole. Once done, it is likely that an explanation will emerge, and that this will form the strategy for further investigation. The reader will receive adequate evidence that will assist them in finding answers to these questions in a book that throws a fascinating light on forensic science and its vital role in the investigation of crime.

Chapter One: The Origins and Role of Forensic Science

Historical Overview

We can trace the dawn of forensic science (as we understand it today) back to 6th century China and the practice of legal medicine. Documents discovered in Chinese archives reference Ti Jen-Chieh, a magistrate who was reputed to have used both logic and forensic evidence to help solve a wide range of crimes. Ti used a team of investigators to study crime scenes, examine physical evidence and interview witnesses and suspects.

The development of forensic science owes much to the ages of scientific discovery taking place during the 16th, 17th and 18th centuries.

Zacharias Janssen invented the 'compound' microscope in 1590. This microscope used a combination of lenses to produce an image significantly larger than the conventional magnifying glass, providing a magnification of some ten times. This technique allowed minute examination of the details of a single fingerprint, to be compared with other prints on record cards or collected from crime scenes.

Complex combinations of more accurately ground lenses were developed during the 17th century. These lenses could produce a magnification of up to three hundred times, enabling forensic scientists to examine hairs, fibres and blood samples, and to make informed decisions as to whether or not one matched another.

By the 1880s, optical microscopes with a magnification of upwards of two thousand times had been developed. In particular, the 'comparison' microscope, which used a two-lens system allowed two images to be viewed side-by-side for direct comparison. This side-by-side observation was ideal for comparing samples such as the marks on two bullets which would indicate whether or not the same gun fired both.

For thousands of years, poison of one sort or another has been the 'weapon' of choice for many killers. With the advantage of a little background knowledge and access to the right materials, a murderer can use a poison to produce symptoms that mimic those of 'natural' killers such as heart disease or pneumonia. However, with the advance in scientific methods, it became more difficult for poison to remain undetected.

In 1814, Matthieu Orfila earned the title of 'father of toxicology' when he published a work entitled *Traite des Poisons*, (Treatise on Poisons), which classified the most common poisons used by criminals at that time.

In 1836, Alfred Swaine Taylor published the monumental textbook, *Elements of Medical Jurisprudence,* which became a classic reference for forensic medicine. In October 1836, English chemist James Marsh, who worked at the Royal Arsenal in Woolwich, London, developed an accurate technique for revealing traces of the poison arsenic. This particular poison was favoured by criminals because it already exists in minute traces in a healthy human body, in organs such as the stomach and liver. A victim of arsenic poisoning will have traces of the chemical distributed in almost every part of the body. These traces remain in the bones and hair of victims even after death, whereas other poisonous substances are broken down by body activity. The <u>*Marsh Test,*</u> as it became known, could reveal a trace of the poison as small as $1/15^{th}$ of a milligram in a sample taken from the body of a victim of a suspicious death.

During the latter part of the 19th century, there was considerable interest shown in trying to identify individuals. One approach studied by Frenchman Alphonse Bertillon was to record and compare facial and limb measurements from individuals convicted of criminal offences. This approach proved to be unsuccessful due to the inherent difficulties in obtaining measurements from a more comprehensive selection of individuals, in particular non-criminals. However, this was the first attempt in a criminal investigation to use a classification system based on scientific measurement.

More successful developments in identification were to emerge from fingerprint examinations. Sir William Herschel (a British civil servant in India) and Henry Fields, were credited with performing most of the early investigations. It was not until 1901 when Sir Edward Henry devised a fingerprint classification scheme for cataloguing and retrieving prints, that the full potential of identification through fingerprint evidence became apparent in forensic investigations.

Body fluid samples have also been found to contain information that can help to identify an individual. The progress made in this particular area has been dramatic, and significant advances have occurred within the past few decades.

Before 1900 it was impossible to determine if a blood sample or stain was of human or animal origin. It was also impossible to classify human blood into four main groups: A, B, AB and O. Even when tests devised by Paul Uhlenhuth (for blood origin) and Karl Landsteiner (for blood grouping) arrived, discrimination between individuals was still relatively weak.

It has only been through recent studies of DNA that dramatic improvements have become apparent when it comes to identifying an individual with confidence. Forensic DNA analysis was first developed in 1984 by Professor (now Sir) Alec Jeffreys at Leicester University in England. He discovered that variations in the human genetic code could identify individuals and distinguish between them.

This process became known as *DNA Fingerprinting* and has now become a significant player in forensic science in assisting in criminal investigations. It is also proving very useful in resolving paternity and immigration disputes.

DNA Fingerprinting was first used by police in Britain to identify the rapist and killer of two teenage girls. They were murdered in Narborough, Leicestershire in 1983 and 1986 respectively. The perpetrator, Colin Pitchfork, was identified and convicted of both murders after samples taken from him matched semen samples taken from the two dead victims.

As a direct result of this case, a National DNA Database was launched in the UK in 1995. This database is now routinely searched by police to match crime-scene DNA profiles to those already stored in the database.

It is to Edmund Locard that the vital principle behind forensic science - *'every contact leaves a trace'* - can be attributed. While the examination of fingerprints or body fluid can directly implicate a person in a crime, other types of trace evidence; glass, paint, gunshot residue can also provide links that establish contact between objects and people involved in a crime or present at a crime scene. Rapid developments in computer technology have played an essential advancement in forensic science. They now permit the storage of vast amounts of data, facilitating quick searches. During the 1970s, the first police national computer (PNC) was developed in Britain which allowed different forces to access a shared bank of criminal records. In 1987, the Home Office in Britain announced the setting up of a major computer system for searching and identifying crime patterns and linking these to known offenders. In a fitting tribute to Sir Arthur Conan Doyle, creator of the famous fictional detective, it was named ***HOLMES*** (Home Office Large Major Enquiry System).

Forensic Science Timeline

1,000 BC: The Chinese use thumbprints to confirm legal documents.

129-216 AD: Galen, Roman physician dissects animals and humans to establish causes of disease.

1194: The post of Coroner first created in Britain.

1200: The first forensic autopsies performed at the University of Bologna, Italy.

1500: Ambroise Pare publishes work on anatomy and military deaths.

1591: Zacharias Janssen designs the first microscope.

1683: Antony van Leeuwenhoek uses a microscope to view living bacteria.

1773: Carl Wilhelm Scheele devises a method for detecting arsenic in dead bodies.

1806: German chemist Valentine Ross expands Scheele's method to detect arsenic.

1810: The first use of document examination in criminal investigations.

1813: Mathieu Orfila publishes the first textbook on Toxicology.

1823: Johannes Purkinje devises first fingerprint classification system.

1836: James Marsh develops a sensitive test for arsenic, *The*

Marsh Test.
1858: Sir William Herschel introduces in thumbprint identification in Bengal, India.
1875: Wilhelm Konrad Rontgen discovers X-Rays.
1876: Cesare Lombroso published *The Criminal Man,* which proposed that criminals could be identified and classified according to their physical characteristics.
1880: Dr Henry Faulds, a Scottish surgeon, demonstrated that powder dusting exposed latent fingerprints. He also proposed a method to record prints using ink.
1882: Frenchman Alphonse Bertillon creates an identification system based on physical measurements of criminals.
1887: The Coroner's Act is passed in England.
1889: Alexandre Lacassagne demonstrates that marks of bullets can be matched to those fired from a rifled barrel.
1892: Sir Francis Galton published a detailed work on fingerprints which became the standard textbook: *Finger Prints.*
1889: Sir Edward Henry devised a fingerprint classification system which formed the basis for those used in Britain and the USA to present day.
1901: Karl Landsteiner formulates the ABO blood typing system.
1904: Oscar and Rudolf Adlar developed the benzidine test for the presence of blood.
1910: Edmund Locard opens the first forensic laboratory in Lyons, France. From Locard comes the basic principle of forensic science: *every contact leaves a trace.* Albert Osborn publishes his *Questioned Documents,* setting out the principles of forensic document analysis.
1925: Philip Gravell and Calvin Goddard develop the comparison microscope.
1953: James Watson, Francis Crick and Maurice Wilkins identify DNA's double-helical structure.
1971: William Bass establishes the Body Farm at Knoxville, Tennessee, USA.
1978: Freeman and Foster develop the ESDA system for Document Analysis.
1984: Sir Alec Jeffreys first develops forensic DNA analysis at Leicester University, England. This analysis proves that variations in the genetic code in humans could identify

individuals.
1985: DNA analysis first applied in a double murder
investigation in Leicestershire, England.
1987: Colin Pitchfork was the first criminal identified by
DNA profiling in the UK.
1990: The Combined DNA Index System was established
(CODIS).
1992: The Polymerase Chain Reaction technique (PCR) first
introduced into DNA analysis.
1994: DNA analysis of Short Tandem Repeats (STR's) first
introduced.

Forensic Science in the United Kingdom

The first police forensic science laboratory in
the United Kingdom was established in 1935 at the
Metropolitan Police headquarters at Hendon, London.
As a result of the success of this laboratory, the Home
Office developed its forensic laboratories under the
banner of the Home Office Forensic Science Service
(FSS). Its purpose was to provide regional
laboratories for police forces in all areas of England
and Wales. These laboratories were financed with
central and local government funds until 1991 when
the Forensic Science Service became an executive
agency of the Home Office. This agency comprised of
five operational laboratories located in Birmingham,
Chepstow, Chorley, Huntingdon and Wetherby.
Agency status enabled the FSS to charge for the
facilities they offered on a contract, case-by-case
basis. These facilities were also available to the
defence in criminal cases. Where work was
performed for both the prosecution and the defence,
this work was carried out at different laboratories to
ensure impartiality. This Agency status allowed the
provision of service to any customer in the UK or
overseas.
Although these five laboratories were
regarded as the 'official' laboratories, there was also a

wide range of practitioners and practices throughout the UK, providing an 'independent' forensic science service to clients via university departments, public analysts and sole practitioners. While these do undertake prosecution work, they also work with lawyers for the defence in criminal cases. However, their primary role is to explore the strength and weaknesses of the scientific evidence submitted by the prosecution. This exploration may involve laboratory examination of 'original' or new material in a case, together with the evaluation of the results obtained by the original forensic scientist.

The FSS's change to agency status, unfortunately, created both 'official' and 'private' laboratories which were all competing against each other for custom from the police, or offering services for the defence. Consequently, it was recognised that there were hidden dangers in a totally 'privatised' forensic science service.

The most apparent dangers were commercial pressures and competition, both of which could lead to compromised standards. Besides, constraints on budgets could also restrict the amount of material submitted and the work performed. The most obvious danger here was that these restraints could prevent the forensic scientists from reaching a conclusion which might provide a court with either more reliable evidence to support a prosecution or demonstrate that the accused could not have committed a criminal act. This unsatisfactory situation is well-described in the article written by Alastair Logan OBE, a distinguished English practising lawyer.

From the early 1990s, forensic science in the UK experienced an open-market in forensic science provision. The FSS competed with private science providers, the FSS holding about 60% of the market in December 2010. It was at this time that the British government announced its intention to wind-down the FSS by March 2012. They stated that the FSS was losing between £1 and £2 million a month, and therefore the service could not be sustained.

Since 2012, forensic science services in England and Wales have been provided to the 43 police forces in England and Wales through a mixture of commercial providers and in-house provision. There are a variety of forensic models adopted which do vary between police forces. However, most of the models use a mixture of in-house and commercial forensic science provisions, arranged in six geographical regions throughout the country.

The Destruction of the Forensic Science Service

"The Forensic Science Service (FSS) was a government-owned company. It provided services to police forces across England and Wales, together with other agencies such as the Crown Prosecution Service, British Transport Police and HM Revenue and Customs. It also provided services to police forces in other countries. Since the early 1990s, the FSS has gradually progressed consequent upon decisions of the governments of the day from a public to a commercial organisation, and a market developed in forensic services with the FSS competing with private forensic science providers (PFSP). The FSS held around 60% market share in December 2010. On 14 December 2010 the government announced its intention to 'support the wind-down of FSS, transferring or selling off as much of its operations as possible' by March 2012. This was disingenuous as it had decided to close the FSS as part of the 2010 spending review. The wording was undoubtedly chosen to deflect any responsibility for the decision to close from government. The decision, taken by those who understand the price of everything but the value of nothing, was vandalism and destroyed an essential pillar underpinning the Criminal Justice System (CJS). The decision to close the FSS was taken without any consultation that one might expect. There are a number of people and bodies that have close connection with the

FSS. They include the government's chief scientific officer Professor Bernard Silverman and the Forensic Science Regulator who is responsible for ensuring the provision of forensic science services across the CJS, and also ensuring that providers have reached and adhere to an appropriate level of scientific quality standards.

Neither was aware of the decision to close the FSS until it was announced. The director of public prosecutions was not consulted, neither was the attorney general nor the lord chief justice. In fact, the only body consulted by the government in advance of its decision to close was the Association of Chief Police Officers (ACPO), a body whose audits carried out over many years have showed consistently poor knowledge and understanding of forensic science. Subsequently the government sought to persuade the Science and Technology Committee of the House of Commons that the reason for closing it was it was losing £2m a month, which the Committee found to be untrue in a damning report produced in June 2011. Why should a constituent part of the CJS have to be profitable? Which other part of the CJS in profitable in financial terms? At a net annual cost of about £12m, the FSS provided a world-class pioneering body that was internationally respected and consulted and was 'a jewel in the crown of the CJS and an exemplary example of value for money'. The bean counters at the Home Office failed to understand that for a body providing a public service the equation is value for funding provided.

We are already back to the old days when police forces such as the Metropolitan Police Service (MPS) had their own in-house forensic laboratories. Some of these had poor-quality standards and their staff were not quality assessed. Moreover they could not be said to be independent, as the FSS was, because they served the force concerned and were not available to or answerable to anyone else. There is a serious concern that some of these laboratories will be "toy labs" where the work done will not be done in accordance with the International Organisation for Standardisation (ISO) 17025, the main ISO standard used by testing and calibration laboratories, as the police will seek to reduce their costs by designating certain work as 'non-forensic' and therefore not needing to be compliant with that accreditation. Thus the collection, collating, classification and processing of samples are likely to be done by people without the relevant accreditation. Indeed, recent press reports suggest that foreign companies will be asked to tender to do this work. Scenes of Crime Officers and their training has been assessed regularly over the last 30 years and this, in common with ACPO, has consistently shown a poor level of understanding of the science and what it could do for them.

One has only to recall the handling of exhibits in the Stephen Lawrence case to know how poor training and understanding affect the detection of crime. Moreover, the focus of the police now is on cost and that will be the determining factor in the application of forensic science to a particular case. The main customer of the private forensic science providers who will now supply the forensic science not done in-house, will be the police themselves. Their interest is to drive down the cost and that will inevitably affect the availability of skills needed to provide forensic science in areas other than DNA and blood analysis. Over 1,600 FSS forensic scientists have been made redundant in the closure and will leave forensic science for good. It is inevitable that some expertise will be lost for ever. Driving down the cost by the largest bulk customer will impact on the cost of forensic science to others such as defendants in the CJS who will not have the clout to get services at a competitive price and who already battling reduced legal aid provision. A survey of forensic scientists carried out by the New Scientist found that 78% of them thought that miscarriages of justice will increase. 70% felt that there will be a reduction in the impartiality of the interpretation of evidence; 65% of them felt that it would make it harder for defence teams to challenge the interpretation of evidence, and a similar number felt that there will be a lessening of openness and transparency by forensic scientists employed by private forensic science providers (PFSP). The single most effective way to ensure that the debris from this act of vandalism is collected and formed into a coherent entity is to give the Forensic Science Regulator statutory powers to regulate this area.

The government, you will not be surprised to learn, does not see the need for this."

Source: Extract from The Law Society Gazette, 22 August 2012. Author: Alastair Logan OBE.

The Role of Forensic Science in the Criminal Justice System

Through a wide range of analytical techniques and scientific disciplines, forensic science plays a vital role in the Criminal Justice System in the UK.

Firstly, by establishing whether or not a crime has been committed, and secondly, by identifying a person of interest through linking the suspect to crime scenes.

Equally important is the elimination of persons from a criminal inquiry, and validating the accounts of witnesses or victims in providing information to link crimes or incidents.

Forensic science helps to establish through time-lines, the sequence of events in a crime, and the cause of death in suspicious deaths.

The Scenes of Crime Officers (SOCO's) undertake initial examination and interpretation of crime scenes to identify relevant forensic evidence which can prove or disprove if a crime has occurred. A crime 'scene' can refer to a specific location, premises, a person or vehicle. The SOCO will search for DNA - relevant material, fingerprints, footprints and any other evidence which will be submitted to a laboratory for examination and analysis.

The police Senior Investigating Officer (SIO) will use the forensic evidence, together with accompanying evidence in the form of witness statements to decide whether to charge a suspect.

Once the case file is passed to the Crown Prosecution Service (CPS), they will assess whether there is sufficient evidence to provide *'a realistic prospect of conviction'*, this being the criterion for prosecution in the UK. A well-used strategy for investigating crime is to focus on six fundamental yet essential questions which require factual answers. These are then evaluated as a whole, the most likely explanation constituting the starting 'hypothesis' which will focus the investigation. These questions are:

What happened?

Where did it happen?
When did it happen?
Who was involved?
How did it happen?
Why did it happen?

We can now consider each of the six fundamental questions.

<u>What</u> is first and foremost concerned with establishing the criminal context and ensuring that the reconstruction of the crime scene is detailed and accurate. This initial question will inevitably give rise to others. What was the sequence of events at the crime scene? Does the pattern of blood staining at the scene suggest an accident or a violent assault? What physical entities were involved in the crime?

<u>Where</u> addresses three connecting issues. Where did the crime take place? Where did objects found at the scene come from? Where else in addition to the scene could they have come from?

<u>When</u> deals with not only the absolute timing of an event but also the sequences within that event. One of the most notable examples of this is the estimation of time of death in the investigation of suspicious deaths. The timing of a recent death within 48 hours, can be estimated from body temperature and the progress of *rigor mortis* (the stiffening of a body). The time of death in older human remains can sometimes be calculated from the stage of infestation of the body by maggots.

<u>Who</u> arises in several situations. Human identity is central to any criminal investigation. The perpetrator of a crime, the victim and witnesses all must be identified. Objective answers emerge from the numerous techniques now used to establish personal identity. These can range from DNA profiling, fingerprints, CCTV imaging, through to

facial reconstruction and finally to the recognition of personal possessions. However, the reliability of personal identification is best when based on immutable characteristics intrinsic to the person, particularly DNA and fingerprints.

How concerns the *modus operandi* or method by which the particular crime was committed. Does the crime under investigation follow a set pattern observed in other similar crimes? If so, it helps to narrow down the police search for likely suspects.

Why, in the sense of a *motive* for the crime can rarely be answered from recovered 'real' evidence. However, it is still a valid point to consider in reconstructing the crime because it also leads to other questions. Why does this look the way it does? And why did the offender carry out a particular action as part of the overall offence? These questions illustrate the value in reconstructing a sequence of events that will provide a holistic view of the crime itself.

"It is a capital mistake to theorise before one has data. One begins to trust facts to suit theories, instead of theories to suit facts."

This quote from Sir Arthur Conan Doyle's Sherlock Holmes story: *The Sign of the Four: A Scandal in Bohemia,* captures the essence of crime scene reconstruction. It contains a warning message about 'twisting facts to suit theories', or following *preconceived* ideas that lack supporting evidence. Good and efficient crime scene reconstruction is a rigorous and challenging, but rewarding process.

By its very nature, forensic science begins at the crime scene, and it is to an examination of the scene that we turn in Chapter Two.

Chapter Two: The Crime Scene

What actually is a 'crime scene'? By definition, it is 'the scene of an incident irrespective of whether a criminal or illegal act has been established'. Should we then consider using the term 'incident scene' rather than 'crime scene'?

Crime Scene Investigation has become a catch-all for the activity. It is of importance that we distinguish between crime scene investigation, crime scene management and crime scene examination, which are all separate activities within the context of crime.

The 'investigation' actually begins with the response to a reported incident and concludes when it is closed. Perhaps the assessment has concluded that there is no sound evidence to suggest that a crime was committed. Alternatively, this may lead to the submission of one or more reports describing what was done, what was discovered, and what conclusions were drawn.

'Scene' investigation is an interactive and collaborative process that can involve police investigators, crime scene officers and specialist forensic science personnel. 'Management' is the process of planning and conducting searches of the crime scene, and 'examination' is the actual conduct of searching and interpreting the scene.

If the crime scene is where the contribution of forensic science begins, then the starting point for the scene itself is the reporting of an incident.

Reporting will occur as a result of a routine police patrol or through an emergency call to the police. The critical first step in the examination of a crime scene is the action taken by the police who respond to the emergency request. It is the role of these 'first officers attending' (or FOA) to evaluate the scene, ensure the safety of any victim, and to determine whether or not a crime may have been committed. If the FOA believe a crime has been committed, a decision then has to be made regarding the correct level of response to initiate. For serious crimes, this will involve contact with detectives and possibly crime scene investigators. If the FOA decides to regard the incident as one of serious crime, then a request will be made for the attendance of a Scenes of Crime Officer (SOCO) and a Senior Investigating Officer (SIO) from the police.

Actions taken at a crime scene are designed to control, preserve, record and recover evidence to allow a reconstruction of the events that created the crime scene.

Control is essentially control of access to the crime scene because there is always a risk that anyone entering the scene may 'contaminate' evidence. For severe and significant crimes, control is implemented by use of cordons. These are the familiar black and yellow tapes displaying: POLICE LINE DO NOT CROSS, or CRIME SCENE DO NOT ENTER. The primary purpose of control is to ensure access to the crime scene is restricted - for reasons of safety, security, integrity and legality.

Control also takes into account these two determining factors. Is the offence a major crime or a volume crime? Is the scene outdoors or indoors? While there is no absolute definition of a major crime, a useful guide is that major crimes are those tried in the Crown Court before a judge and jury. These usually involve the most serious crimes such as murder and rape. Volume crimes are the more common offences including assault, house-breaking and criminal damage, typically dealt with at the

Magistrates' Courts. It is interesting to note that DNA databases have shown that offenders of major crimes are often also the perpetrators of volume crimes.

Indoor crime scenes tend to be more straightforward, as the integrity of the scene is protected against most environmental influences. Outdoor crime scenes are much more difficult to control and preserve.

Preserving the scene from contamination is the one element that often features in fictional TV crime dramas, but it is factually correct regarding the use of protective clothing. These overalls are usually white and made from TYVEK, which is a robust and breathable polyethylene fibre. The protective clothing is worn with examination gloves, face masks, and footwear covers. All these prevent any transfer of traces such as fibres and DNA between examiners and the scene and vice-versa. Preserving the crime scene from the environment is usually necessary when the scene is located outdoors and needs protection from the weather. The erection of portable tents secures such sites.

Recording a crime scene is necessary to create a permanent repository of knowledge about its particulars. Such records are an essential requirement for legal purposes, report writing and reconstruction of the scene during the investigation and sometimes at a later date. Such records establish contemporaneous accounts of the investigation at the time it was conducted. They typically include notes, plans, diagrams and witness statements, supported by still and video photography. Also, these can be supplemented by other specialist techniques such as aerial, underwater and panoramic images. Finally, all items of interest will be photographed *in situ* before being collected. These will include fingerprints, footwear and tool-mark impressions and blood patterns.

Recover involves identifying and recovering items of potential evidential interest from searching the scene. Effective scene searching is a planned and systematic process.

There are two kinds of evidential material. One is individual and unique to the scene, such as pieces of a broken object, tool marks, bullets or fingerprints. The other is identifiable but not unique, such as fibres from a piece of clothing or fragments of paint or glass.

Whatever the nature of the evidence, it is essential that the 'chain of custody' is maintained and recorded. Different items of evidence inevitably pass between people, and each movement of the evidence must be logged and signed for. Otherwise, the defence in a case may be justified in questioning the validity of the evidence. The purpose of what may appear to be a repetitive procedure is to ensure that when the evidence is presented in court, the court will be satisfied that a piece of evidence being discussed at the trial is the same evidence that was retrieved from the crime scene.

The Scenes of Crime Officer's role at the scene is the discovery and recovery of evidence such as DNA, fingerprints and footprints. Each SOCO carries out their own enquiries and assessments on the points of the scene that require examination. At the end of the scene examination, the SOCO will have:

1. Recorded all the features of the scene by diagram, notes and photographs.
2. Searched the scene, recovered and recorded all the 'physical' evidence.
3. Packed all the evidence in secure and labelled

containers.
4. Looked for and recovered all traces left by the offender.
5. Taken 'control samples' of all the materials the offender could have taken from the scene.
6. Formed a clear impression of how the crime had been committed.

When police are faced with a major crime incident or series of crimes, the sheer size of the task and the numbers involved introduce complex management and communication issues. A Senior Investigating Officer (SIO) controls the enquiry with a management team to which all information is directed. This information is controlled and stored through an 'incident' room using a computer system known as HOLMES, which is an abbreviation for the Home Office Large Major Enquiry System. The relevant police force's Scientific Support Department will put into place its own management structure to manage both resources and the demands of the enquiry.

Crime Scene Personnel – Flow Chart	
FIRST OFFICER AT THE SCENE (FOA)	
Volume Crime Scene	**Major Crime Scene**
Scenes of Crime Officer (SOCO) Police Investigating Officer (CID)	Senior Investigating Officer (SIO) Crime Scene Manager (CSM) Scientific Support Officer (SSO) Senior Forensic Scientist

The Crime Scene Manager (CSM) will exercise judgement over all the key activities of the department.

An Exhibits Officer will be responsible for control, continuity and security of all exhibits.

If the enquiry is a complex one, a Scientific Support Co-ordinator (SSO) will be part of the team to oversee the combined scientific support to the enquiry.

In cases of murder or suspicious death, the first person to examine a body will usually be a police surgeon. It is their responsibility to establish whether the person is, in fact, dead. The police will usually only get involved if the doctor notices anything suspicious. In such cases, the doctor is obliged to report the matter to the local Coroner.

The Coroner's duty is to hold an Inquest which is an independent investigation into the cause of death. However, there are some cases of 'suspicious' death which are automatically regarded as suspicious under English law. These include the sudden death of young people previously not known to have a life-threatening illness. Post-mortem examinations are obligatory in all cases of suspicious deaths.

Deciding to call a forensic scientist to a crime scene depends on the practical needs of the physical evidence and the complexity of the case. Such a call-out may occur where particular forms of evidence are present. Patterns of blood-staining, foot marks and other marks on bodies, and firearms residue and discharge would require a forensic scientist's assistance.

It is the Senior Investigating Officer (SIO) and the Crime Scene Manager (CSM) who influence the direction and priorities of the criminal investigation.

Three working examples of specialist forensic involvement will now be examined to enable readers to appreciate and compare the different forensic approaches to these investigations. These are a firearms incident, a fire investigation and finally, an explosion investigation.

Firearms Incident

The specialist firearms investigator's assistance at the scene of a shooting incident, especially if death has occurred, is both valuable and indispensable. It involves working side by side with the investigating team, and with the pathologist at the post-mortem examination. The considerable activity which commonly accompanies a shooting scene and the nature of the operation of the weapon requires accurate recording of the scene by document, photography and sketch. Close-up photography of wounds, bloodstains and the relative position of injuries, bullet holes, cartridge cases or shot damage is essential. Examining a shooting incident's scene provides information about the type of weapon used and the distance over which it was fired, together with the positions of the firer and the victim. It will indicate whether the incident which occurred was an accident, a suicide or murder. Information from residue on clothing and skin, together with scale photographs of marks and injuries, can be linked by test-firing the weapon to estimate the range and direction of a shot. The accurate reconstruction of the scene using all available evidence provides valuable information about lines of fire, the position of the victim(s), the firing position of the perpetrator and their various movements.

Fire Incident

An excellent example of a multi-disciplinary team approach to crime scene investigation involves the forensic scientist who specialises in fire investigation. The investigation of arson and fatal fires, and their differentiation from accidental causes, requires expertise based on extensive practical experience in this field of science, together with a sound knowledge of fire science and laboratory analysis.

The investigation team may consist of fire brigade officers, police officers, scientific support officers, forensic scientists and, where fatalities are involved, pathologists. The fire officer will initially seek to identify the causes and seat of the fire. His suspicions are not proof, but he must be aware of the correct steps to preserve evidence. The police officer will initiate the investigation but will require the technical input of a Scientific Support Officer with the necessary background and experience.

These three will decide whether the cause of the fire is self-evident, whether the cause may be evident by analysis of possible incendiary materials, or whether a forensic scientist attending the scene will help to determine the cause. Each member of the team will give evidence only in their own area of expertise when the case eventually comes to court.

Explosion Incident

The investigation of the crime scene after an explosion is totally different from other types of scene because of the nature of the incident. While trace evidence will still be present, it will have been dispersed by force of the explosion from the source or centre of the blast, and the severity of the explosion can cause damage ranging from localised destruction with a window blown out, to the destruction of substantial buildings. In investigation terms, these may be considered as 'non-terrorist' or 'terrorist' offences.

Non-terrorist offences arise from an accidental or deliberate act where a blast is produced by the ignition of gas, flammable vapours and combustible dusts, or by the sudden release of pressure where a sealed container explodes. The cause can range from leaking gas in a domestic situation to an incident in an industrial plant. In these cases, which may be caused deliberately, by accident, or through negligence, the investigator follows the 'team' approach of fire investigation. The team approach involves the addition of specialist investigators from the government Health and Safety Executive or public utilities such as gas or electricity as appropriate. In such cases, scene disturbance to recover the dead or injured, or to make the scene safe, doesn't interfere with determining the cause of the explosion).

If the cause of the explosion is a deliberate act, then any suspect will be treated as a crime scene to recover trace evidence from their clothing and person. Where terrorist activity is suspected possibly following the operation of an explosive device, the initial action taken is to contain and secure the scene. Safety takes precedence over all other issues, and specialist advice is sought, although the scene may be disturbed by emergency services in their effort to save lives.

Initially, a Bomb Scene Manager will take control of the scene advised by specially trained military personnel, Scientific Support Officers, and Anti-Terrorist Police Officers. When the scene is considered safe, a search will be done for traces of explosive material and the components of the explosive device itself. The latter may well be shattered into fragments over a large area. After clearing a common approach path to provide access, the scene will be divided into zones and searched systematically. The force of the explosion will cause evidence not only to be dispersed but also to be embedded in walls, ceilings, furniture or people and thrown onto rooftops.

Although some hand searching may be carried out, it is necessary to remove much debris in large containers. Contents will later be sieved and carefully searched by specialists at the appropriate forensic science laboratory. Fragments found may, when analysed, indicate both the type of device and composition and source of explosive used. The handling of clothing and property of someone suspected of having been in contact with explosives requires an exceptionally high level of cleanliness and control. Because of the risk of contamination, the Scientific Support Officers wear disposable protective clothing and keep themselves and suspects separate from areas in police stations, vehicles or indeed from other officers where these may have been in contact with firearms, explosives or ammunition. One area of concern at crime scenes is the issue of Health and Safety. Where body fluids are present, post-mortems are carried out. When buildings are unsafe through fire or explosion, these are areas of risk, so the Scientific Support Officer must be aware, and must be mindful of alerting others. It is, however, particularly important that a forensic scientist should be consulted and attend all aspects of the investigation of premises involved in the illicit manufacture of drugs, where the hazards might range from inhalation, or contact with noxious chemicals, to the risk of fire or explosion.

Suspicious Deaths

On receiving information of a 'suspicious' death or possible murder, one of the advantages for an investigator is that police forces in the UK have an established *Serious Crime Procedure.* The procedure enables most of the elements for the initial investigation to be put in place quickly. In such cases, the <u>victim</u> is regarded as the 'crime scene', and a post-mortem will have been performed.

The team assembled for a post-mortem examination consists of the pathologist, mortuary technicians and the Scientific Support Officer who will record the procedure by photographs and video recording and will receive packages and label exhibits ranging from clothing to body samples for analysis. The pathologist will take all relevant samples from the body, and then make a full exploration of any injuries before concluding with a detailed internal examination of the body. A Scientific Support Officer will take finger, palm and foot impressions if appropriate.

At the conclusion of the post-mortem, the Senior Investigating Officer (SIO) will ask the pathologist for a cause of death, and to classify it as 'accident', suicide', 'murder' or ' natural causes'. The nature and direction of the criminal investigation is entirely dependent upon this decision. To satisfy legal requirements in England and Wales, a Coroner must be informed of the death and assumes responsibility for the body until it is released for burial or cremation.

The Real CSI: What happens at a crime scene?

On 19 February 2001, a bag was found in London's Regent Canal, containing the dismembered corpse of a 32-

year-old woman, Paula Fields. She was a mother of three who had become involved in drugs and prostitution. Police eventually linked the crime to John Sweeney, who was captured in March 2001, after seven years on the run for trying to kill girl friend, Delia Balmer. Thanks to new DNA evidence, Sweeney was linked to another crime; the 1990 murder of an American woman named Melissa Halstead, whose body was found in the Westersingel Canal in Rotterdam. On 4 April 2011, Sweeney was given a 'whole life' sentence for the murders of Fields and Halstead.

John Cockram, Crime Scene Manager

"The anticipation kicks in as soon as I get the call. I get in the car, put on some classical music and start thinking. Every crime scene is different. It's nowhere near what you expect. When I arrive, I get a briefing from whoever's at the scene. You listen but you don't necessarily agree. I call it ABC; assume nothing, believe nobody, check everything. Maybe, it's the first time a police officer has seen a body. They'll give a fantastic description of a decomposing corpse, but I can see that with my own eyes. I'll ask: did you smell anything? Did the key come flying out? I'm trying to get them to see further than the body on the floor. When I arrive at a scene, it's my thinking time. It's now sterile. The circus hasn't arrived, so I get suited up and go in with my notepad. What am I seeing? What am I hearing? I tend to follow the left-hand wall around a room. It's a good technique. Blood distribution, saliva, little bits and pieces, I'm not going to miss it. Which lights are on? Which are off? Has the toilet been flushed? Is the seat up or down?

I can remember virtually every job, I've done about 100 murder scenes and 200 suspicious deaths. When it comes to cordons, I always think big. A cordon can always shrink afterwards because people have to get on with their lives, so you can't cordon off a whole estate. How am I going to manage the situation without compromising the evidence? With the Paula Fields case, you've' got five bags in a canal, two entry points. Questions arise: who's going to carry five bags? How man people? In fact there was one person. How heavy are the bags? Has he brought a car here? The bags were weighed down with brick and tiles. I notice a skip nearby, perhaps that should be part of my crime scene. Most importantly, how am I going to deal with these body parts? I've got people from nearby offices looking out of the window at what I'm doing. All these things run through your head.

You have to make a decision as to what you're going to get out of a scene, how much of detail you're to look at when you're at the mortuary or the laboratory. You need to be able to effectively reconstruct the crime scene at the court afterwards. Maybe, 70% of what you retrieved is not relevant. That doesn't stop you finishing with a fingertip search, looking for that last piece of detail. I'm the conductor of an orchestra. I don't need to know how to play the violin, but I need to know what sound they make and, more importantly, when to bring them in, to recognise when I need a blood pattern analysis expert, a forensic archaeologist, a pathologist, a biologist which are pollen experts, an environmental scientist. I have to bring then to the scene at the correct time and usually deal with egos. They're experts: they come to a scene and think they've got answers to everything. They haven't. They're just a cog in the machine. On the canal bank, I asked myself, what am I going to do with these bags? Can I get a pathologist to the scene now? When is the post-mortem going to happen? These things all add up in your mind. We should do something here now, I decided. We got a big tent in and got started. We look for finger marks, hairs, fibres, obviously, but in this case we also looked at the plastic bin liners that held the remains. If you find a roll of plastic bags at a suspect's address, you can prove where the bag has come from. You need to know this sort of thing. You've only got one chance. If you seize the wrong things to start with, no matter how well you manage the people, the budget, the egos, then you're lost".
Source: Extract from *The Guardian,* 27 April 2012 – Author Craig Taylor.

Chapter Three: Time of Death

When was the murder committed is one of the most frequently asked questions in any murder investigation. There is a common perception that estimating the time of death is a routine process. In fact, it is probably the most difficult of all questions during a murder investigation.

At its basic level, at death, the human body begins to cool down, and this rate of cooling and time is well understood. Under 'room' conditions, a body will lose heat at the rate of approximately $1.5°$ F per hour during the first six hours following death. There will be a slight slowing of cooling over the following twelve hours at the rate of between $1-1.5°$ F per hour. After twenty-four hours since death, the body temperature will have reached that of the 'ambient' or surrounding air temperature. The body will under 'normal' circumstances feel cold to the touch approximately twelve hours after death. However, there are exceptions to this normal progression of body cooling. For example, if the deceased died from asphyxiation (strangulation) or cerebral haemorrhage (bleeding on the brain), the initial temperature at death may be raised above the normal temperature of $98.6°$ F.

It is also well understood that a naked body will cool more rapidly than a clothed body, as would one immersed in water. Also, a larger-built individual would lose heat more slowly than a slightly- built person. It is usual practice in forensic medicine to establish the body temperature of the deceased *in situ* before removal to a mortuary. Also, the ambient temperature at the scene is taken to establish a relationship between the two.

A recurring problem is the requirement to

establish the time of death within the limits of 'probability'.

As a result, the more time elapsed between death and the discovery and examination of the body, the more extensive are the limits of probability. Also, the time of death has legal significance, in particular to the questions of 'alibi' and 'opportunity'.

For example, if a suspect can prove that he or she was at some other location when the fatal injury was inflicted on the deceased, then they have an alibi, and their innocence is therefore implicit. On the other hand, if at the time of a fatal assault, a suspect was known to have been in the vicinity of the victim, then the suspect had the opportunity to commit the crime.

Algor mortis (the medical definition for body-cooling) is the most useful single indicator of the time of death during the first 24 hours after death. However, it is essential to point out that the use of body temperature applies only to 'cool and temperate' climates. Consequently, in tropical regions, there may occur a minimal fall in body temperature, and in some extreme climates, the temperature may even rise after death.

The assessment of time since death is made using calculations that use the body core temperature. This temperature is ascertained by using a rectal thermometer of approximately 10 to 12 inches in length. It is usually assumed that the body temperature at death is normal, which in most circumstances can fluctuate between 96.7 and 99° F. The two important unknowns in assuming time of death from body temperature are (a) the 'actual' body temperature at time of death and (b) the actual length of the post-mortem interval (PMI). It is for this reason that assessment of time of death from body temperature cannot be accurate during the first four or five hours after death when these two unknown factors are most relevant. In addition, body temperature cannot be a useful guide to time of death once the body of the deceased reaches that of the ambient, surrounding temperature. Nonetheless, during the intervening period, any formula which involves an average of temperature cooling per hour may provide a reasonably reliable estimate of time of death.

The most common method for determining a person's time of death using body temperature is that of *Moritz's Formula*. This formula states that the body cools at the rate of 1.5° F per hour for the first 12 hours, and then 1° F per hour for the next 12 hours. Assuming that the body temperature was normal at 98.6° F, this figure minus the rectal temperature, divided by 1.5° F will give an approximate number of hours since the death. For example, if the deceased was examined at 6.00 pm and their core rectal temperature was found to be 92° F, then using the Moritz Formula, it can be established that the person had died at approximately 1.36 PM that same day.

The calculations for this approximation would be as follows:

$$\frac{\text{Normal Temperature} \quad \text{Core Rectal Temperature}}{1.5° \text{F}}$$
$$98.6 °\text{F} \qquad\qquad 92° \text{F}$$

Hours since death = 4. 4 hours

The numerator (upper figures) indicate how many degrees F the body temperature has decreased. The instance above indicates a decrease of 6.6° F. When this is divided by 1.5° F (the rate of cooling per hour for the first six hours), this gives a figure of 4.4,

the approximate number of hours that have elapsed
since death. To change the 4 hours to minutes, this is
multiplied by 60 minutes per hour, giving a figure of
24 minutes. The hours since death are subtracted from
the time when the body temperature was taken at 6.00
pm. Thus, we arrive at an approximate time of death:

6pm minus 4 hours = 2pm minus 24 minutes = 1.36pm

A forensic medical examiner would give an
approximate time of death 'plus or minus' an hour,
either way, putting the death at probably between
12.30 and 2.30 pm. The reader can now appreciate
that 'cooling' rate is the 'classic' method for
estimating the time of death, at least in the early
stages. However, it is important to remember that this
method can only be applied to a maximum of
between 20 and 24 hours post-mortem.

Livor Mortis (also known as 'post-mortem
lividity' or hypostasis) results in the appearance of
reddish-purple patches on the skin of the deceased.
This change occurs because, after death, the blood
ceases to circulate. Due to the laws of gravity, it sinks
to those parts of the body that are lowermost.

For example, a dead body found lying face
down, would display lividity on the abdomen, where
one lying on its back would display lividity patches
on the back and back of the thighs. Those parts of the
body that are compressed against the ground will
display a white area since the blood vessels are
unable to refill.

Livor mortis appears within 2 hours after
death and becomes more widespread after about 4-5
hours. At this point, the initial patches of lividity fuse
together to form a continuous discoloured area of
skin. However, lividity is a limited guide to time since

death. The medico-legal importance lies in its colour and distribution. Lividity is first evident about 20-30 minutes after death. After 10-12 hours the lividity becomes fixed then fades very slowly but not completely. Fading of the primary pattern of lividity and the development of a secondary pattern will be quicker and more complete if the body is moved within the first 6 hours. This duality of distribution of lividity is a crucial forensic factor because it demonstrates that the body of the deceased had been moved after death. This factor would arouse suspicion.

For lividity to have forensic value, the body must have remained in one position for about 10 hours. Only then will the lividity be well developed enough. Most medico-legal textbooks agree that lividity attains its maximum intensity around 12 hours post-mortem. Under normal circumstances, death is followed immediately by muscular relaxation termed 'primary muscular flaccidity'. This relaxation is followed by generalised muscular stiffening or *Rigor Mortis*. After a 'variable' period, this passes off spontaneously followed by secondary muscular flaccidity.

In temperate climates, rigor will typically start to disappear at about 36-48 hours after death. However, if the environmental temperature is high, then the development of putrefaction or decomposition may completely displace rigor mortis within 9-12 hours of death. However, there is considerable variation in the rate of onset and duration of rigor mortis. As a general rule, when the onset of rigor is rapid, then its duration is relatively slow.

The two main factors influencing the onset and duration of rigor are (a) the environmental temperature and (b) the degree of muscular activity before death. The onset of rigor is accelerated, and its duration shortened when the environmental temperature is high. Rigor is rapid in onset and of short duration after prolonged muscular activity such as fighting. Also, the onset is relatively more rapid in children and the elderly than in muscular young adults.

One rule of thumb offered by the late Professor Francis Camps, the eminent English forensic pathologist was; "*corpses can usually be divided into those still warm, in which the 'rigor' is still present, indicating death within about three hours. Those in which 'rigor' is progressing, death probably having occurred between two and nine hours previously. Those in which rigor is fully established, show that death occurred more than nine hours previously*".

Conversely, Professor Bernard Knight, another notable English forensic pathologist, has stated that "*the only possible use (of rigor mortis) is in the period around the second day, when body temperature may have dropped to that of the environment but putrefaction has not yet occurred. If full 'rigor' is present, then one might assume that this is about the second day following death, depending upon the environmental conditions*".

'Cadaveric spasm' is an instantaneous 'rigor' which occurs at the precise moment of death and persists into the period of 'rigor mortis'. This phenomenon is usually associated with violent deaths in circumstances of intense emotion. It does have a medico-legal significance in that it records the 'last act of life' of the individual.

Such a spasm can affect all the muscles of the body, but it is most commonly experienced in certain groups of muscles only, such as those of the forearm and hands. Should an object be held in the hand such as a gun or knife, the cadaveric spasm will cause the hand to become firmly wrapped around the object. This phenomenon is seen in a small proportion of suicidal deaths from firearms and stab wounds. In such circumstances, the gripping of the weapon creates a presumption of self-infliction of the injury.

Of forensic importance is the fact that this state cannot be reproduced <u>after</u> death by placing a weapon in the hands of the victim. It is also seen in cases of drowning when the victim clutches grass weeds and other materials. In these circumstances, it provides proof of the existence of life at the time the victim entered the water. In some homicide cases, hair or clothing from the assailant may be found in the hands of the victim.

Putrefaction or decomposition of the body can provide some indicators as to the time of death. Approximately two days after death, a 'marbling' pattern appears at the neck and runs down the arms and sides of the abdomen. Initially, this appears as red before turning green later. These changes are the result of bacteria already in the body tissues invading the blood vessels. The body then becomes 'bloated' through gas generated by bacterial metabolism, the external feature of the body becoming unrecognisable.

This bloating is a sign that the internal organs are decomposing, and the order in which this occurs can give some indication as to the time of death. The stomach, heart and liver begin to decompose first. They are followed by the lungs, brain and spinal cord, and finally, the sexual organs break down. These are the main changes in the body that can 'broadly' indicate the time of death.

'Forensic Entomology' is the study of insects in a legal context. The most frequent application is to determine the <u>minimum</u> time since death or the post-mortem interval (or PMI) in investigations of a suspicious death. This investigation is done by identifying the age of the insects present on a human body. This can provide a relatively precise estimate in circumstances where pathologists may only be able to offer a broad approximation. The fundamental assumption is that the body has not been dead for longer than it took the insects to arrive at a corpse and develop. Thus, the age of the 'oldest' insects on the body, determine the minimum PMI. The insects of the greatest value to forensic entomology are the blowflies (*Calliphoridae)* because they are usually the first insects to colonise a body after death - often within hours.

The age of the oldest blowflies gives the most accurate evidence of the PMI. There are many other species of insects that visit a dead body, but they tend to arrive after the blowflies so are less useful in establishing the PMI.

Adult blowflies are well adapted to sensing and locating the sources of smells of decay. Their eggs are usually laid in the natural orifices of a human body such as eyes, nose, mouth and ears. The eggs hatch into 'first instar larvae' that grow rapidly as maggots. They progress through second and third instars until they finish feeding off the body. Depending on the particular species, they pupate on the body or move away to another suitable site. The larva then contracts, and the cuticle hardens and darkens to form a barrel-shaped puparium within which the pupa metamorphoses into an adult fly. The rate of development of all insects is directly dependent on the ambient conditions, especially temperature.

Between upper and lower thresholds which vary between species, the higher the temperature, the faster the insects develop, and the lower the temperature, the slower they will develop. If the ambient temperatures during the period of development are known, then, in theory, the minimum PMI can be determined.

The degree to which a forensic entomologist is involved in a case can vary. The entomologist may attend the crime scene to collect the insect specimens from the body or its surroundings. This procedure is ideal because he or she can use knowledge of insect biology to ensure that as many examples as possible are collected, potentially increasing the accuracy of results.

When investigating a suspicious death, four main questions require answers.

Which <u>species</u> of blowfly are present on the body? The collected specimens must be correctly identified to ensure that all relevant information on physiological, behaviour and ecology of that insect species can be used.

Which are the <u>oldest</u> specimens of blowfly? They may still be feeding on the body; they may have left the body to pupate elsewhere, or they may have already emerged as adults and left behind their empty puparial cases.

How old are the <u>oldest</u> specimens? Estimating age involves the detailed morphological study of the insects under a binocular microscope, to determine their 'stage of development' and to compare that with data from standard databases relating to the developmental stage to age at different temperatures.

What were the <u>ambient temperatures</u> at the scene while the flies were developing on the body?

An electronic temperature data logger is placed at the crime scene for seven to ten days, and the readings are compared with data from the meteorological station over the same period. This comparison of data from the time before the discovery of the body can then be used to estimate the temperature during that period at the scene of the crime. This determines the temperature at which the larvae developed.

What other factors affect the decomposition of a body in a way that can assist with determining the time of death? It is well known that humidity speeds decomposition while dry conditions retard it. In buried bodies, it is believed that soil pH (the degree of acidity or alkalinity) does not affect the rates of decomposition of a body. However, this belief is open to criticism. The time of death of buried bodies can be estimated by studying the *fauna* involved in burials.

The fauna found in the soil beneath a buried body (one buried without a coffin) and therefore classed as a 'clandestine' burial, will change in specific, predictable ways. The existing fauna will decrease both in the number of species and individuals. This occurs because the decaying body releases highly toxic decomposition products. As a result, the fauna slowly disappears, taking up to two months to complete.

This loss is followed by a new fauna which will be different from the original fauna at the site of burial, and will gradually develop to its maximum extent. The exact order of events depends upon the nature of the soil and the time of year.

One of the main biological events occurring in soil is the growth of plant roots. It can happen that sometimes the roots of a tree penetrate through the skeletons of a buried body. Knowledge of the speed of development of particular plants can assist in time of death calculations, just as the number of 'growth rings' in damaged roots can assist in the calculation of the time of burial.

Taphonomy, the patterns of bone scattering can also give a 'general' indication of the time of death of a body. This is because of the correlation between time of death and the extent of the disarticulation and scattering of bones. Bone scattering is believed to begin around five weeks after death. However, this will depend largely on local conditions, such as the species of wild animal present in the location of the grave.

This chapter has examined the forensic techniques employed by scientists to estimate the time of death - the "When?" of a criminal investigation. The following chapter describes the 'causes of death'(the "how?" of criminal investigation) and centres on the more usual methods by which crimes are committed.

Chapter Four: The Causes of Death

Forensic pathologists distinguish between the 'cause' of death and the 'manner' of death. The 'cause' of death might be specified as heart failure, while the 'manner' of death may be the result of a stabbing to the heart. In such circumstances, the manner of death would be the 'cause' of the cause of death. 'Violent' death can be described as the 'mode' of death, which describes the 'way' the person actually died. In a criminal investigation, this raises the question, was this a 'natural' death, a suicide or a murder?

Mode or Manner of Death

[1] Stabbing

Stabbing someone to death with a sharp-tipped instrument is still a widespread mode of murder. By definition, a stab wound is a deep penetrating wound. However, it should be remembered that not all stabbings are inflicted with sharp instruments. In fact, blunt instruments such as a screwdriver, closed scissors or a poker can also inflict severe wounds.

As a general rule, the blunter the instrument used, the more 'ragged' will be the 'entry' wound, and more 'bruised' will be the skin surrounding the entry. When a particularly sharp knife is used in a stabbing incident, the entry wound may appear as a small slit in the skin. So a single-edged kitchen knife will leave a slit that tapers towards one end.

However, the shapes of entry wounds can vary according to the 'method' used to stab. If the victim twists or the assailant turns the knife on stabbing, then the entry wound will change in appearance. Such action would make it difficult to estimate the 'width' of the knife blade used in the attack. When it comes to assessing the 'length' of the knife blade, this will be the 'minimum' length because the blade may not have punctured the body right up to the hilt. However, the 'depth' of the cut will give a measure of the minimum length of the blade. The way a stab is inflicted can indicate as to whether the wound was self-inflicted or not.

In those cases where a victim's throat is cut, several indications point to the death as being a suicide or a murder. It is well-observed in forensic medicine that suicides <u>never</u> kill themselves with just one single clean cut to the throat. There will be evidence of several 'trial' cuts before the final, fatal cut is inflicted. These several cuts to the throat will usually be found to be initially shallow in depth, appearing very close together, and running almost parallel to each other. These are usually located on the throat side opposite to the hand that is typically used for writing. For a right-handed person, the cuts would be found on the left-hand side of the throat. The final or fatal cut will be deep and traverse downwards, then across the throat and upwards in the general direction of the opposite ear.

It has been found that such wounds can be very deep, with knife-cutting strokes going through to the spine.

In homicidal throat-cutting, the cuts appear fewer and more cleanly incised, with a noticeable absence of 'trial' cuts. In addition, a noticeable characteristic of homicidal cutting is that the cuts inflicted will be higher or lower than those found in suicides. Also, the victim's hands will often be injured, providing evidence of 'defence' wounds.

[2] Asphyxiation

Death by strangulation is due to asphyxia, a word derived from the Greek, meaning 'absence of pulsation'. In forensic terms, this means 'interference with oxygenation'. The mechanisms of death in such cases is simply 'lack of oxygen'.

The biochemical changes that occur include a decrease of oxygen in the blood and tissues and an increase in carbon dioxide. This results in the development of a purplish colouration of the skin known as *cyanosis. Petechiae* or spots of haemorrhage appear which are due to the bursting of minute blood vessels. The petechial haemorrhages are an excellent indicator of asphyxia.

However, one exception is when the 'vagus' nerve is inhibited due to pressure being applied to it during the process of strangulation. This can cause death quite quickly and suddenly. Asphyxia can be caused in several ways, including accidental choking on food.

A more common form of death caused by asphyxiation is drowning. When someone drowns, the air passages together with the stomach, are filled with water. People who drown in 'natural' bodies of water will often have large numbers of microscopic algae with silicon shells called *diatoms* in their blood, bone marrow and brain. From a medico-legal perspective, the presence of these diatoms is evidence that the victim was still alive when they entered the water. The use of diatoms as a diagnostic test for drowning is based on the hypothesis that they will not enter the body via the circulatory system unless it is still functioning.

Not all water deaths are, in fact, drownings. *'Vagal'* inhibition is caused by a sudden change in body temperature, such as falling or being thrown into icy water. Loss of consciousness is usually instantaneous, and death follows within minutes. The cause is believed to be 'cardiac arrest' induced by cold water. The mechanisms of drowning (the inhalation and swallowing of water) result in a catastrophic disturbance in the osmotic balance of the body. Drowning in fresh water is usually very rapid because the blood becomes diluted, and water enters the blood cells, which cause bursting. However, in 'sea water' drowning is much slower because osmotic pressure in the blood is increased, resulting in water flowing out of the blood cells.

These are important characteristics of drowning which can provide valuable forensic clues to the circumstances surrounding the case.

Drowned persons who are found 'unclothed' or in swimming clothes are very likely to have drowned 'accidentally'. Those drowned fully-clothed are more likely to have done so by intent or as a result of criminal activity. Suicides tend to remove some clothing before entering the water, and deep water is often chosen for such purposes.

Hanging is a particular 'manner' of death of which asphyxia is a component. Hanging can, in fact, be described as having two 'manners' of death. A 'judicial' hanging or execution involves a long drop that breaks the cervical vertebrae in the neck. A 'suicidal' hanging, on the other hand, can cause death in three distinct ways. Firstly, pressure on the jugular veins and carotid arteries in the neck results in deprivation of oxygen to the brain. Secondly, the pressure on the 'vagus' nerve, which is the tenth 'cranial' nerve that controls the muscles of swallowing, causes breathing inhibition. Finally, asphyxia results because the breathing passageways are obstructed by the tongue and glottis which are forced in the pharynx. Victims of hanging display the same post-mortem signs as those of strangulation, so cyanosis and petechiae are present. But in cases of hanging, ligature marks are present on the neck.

[3] Blunt Instruments

Blunt instruments are often used as weapons in assault and murder and can inflict severe injuries to the victim. As a general rule, assaults with a blunt instrument are usually aimed towards the head of a victim. Consequently, death is often the result of brain injuries. For a blunt instrument to be effective, it must have two specific attributes, its <u>weight</u> and the <u>speed</u> in which it is used. The resultant force of the blow is referred to as its *kinetic energy.* This refers to the speed with which the instrument is travelling at the time of contact with its victim, which will create the greatest effect. For example, a heavy blow with a piece of timber will cause more injury to a victim than a light blow with a hammer.

It is a fact that blunt instruments are the most dangerous of weapons. Attacks involving the use of such weapons result in widespread blood loss at a crime scene. Several well-aimed powerful blows will undoubtedly kill a victim. Once such a blow shatters the skull, it will inevitably result in damage to the brain of the victim. In fact, any blow to the head, including that of a fist, can result in brain damage because of the free movement of the brain within the skull cavity.

A specific type of head injury is known as the *contrecoup,* and it occurs when the head strikes the ground after a fall. In such instances, the injury occurs at a spot that is opposite to that at which the head was struck. For example, if a man falls backwards striking the back of his head on the ground, a striking injury may be seen at the front of his brain over the roof of his eye sockets. The injury might be revealed by the development of black eyes.

[4] Firearms

Firearms are of two types - smooth-bore and rifled weapons. Smooth-bored weapons or shotguns, have barrels that are smooth on the inside and fire *shot-pellet*s, not bullets. The barrel is usually tapered towards the muzzle end, to keep the pellets together when they are discharged. Rifled weapons are not smooth inside the barrel, which is spirally scored or *rifled.* This is to ensure that the bullet rotates as it travels through the barrel and outside. This mechanism helps to stabilise the bullet in its flight and to travel on a straight course for up to 1,000 metres. The inside of the barrel will be made up of spiral bands known as the *lands*, and indented spiral bands called the *grooves*. Rifles, revolvers and pistols are all 'rifled' weapons which fire bullets. The *calibre* of a gun is its diameter from land to land. Hence the types .303 and .45 refer to this diameter.

Bullets fired from a particular gun will display markings that correspond to the 'rifling' of the weapon from which it was fired. No two guns are identical, even those made by the same manufacturer in succession. It is possible to compare a bullet discovered at a crime scene or recovered from the body of a victim, with a bullet experimentally fired from a suspect gun. This procedure will reveal conclusively whether a bullet was fired from that particular weapon.

In forensic investigations, it is often necessary to restore the 'serial' number that manufacturers stamp on a gun. This restoration can assist in helping to trace the 'history' of a particular weapon. From a general point of view, most textbooks state that the 'exit' wound of a bullet is much larger than that of the 'entry' wound. However, this is not always the case, depending on the nature of the bullet and the part of the body involved.

In principle, when a bullet enters a body and emerges, the entry wound can be larger than the exit wound, if it is a 'normal' bullet moving through flesh. However, this rarely happens because most bullets hit bone at some stage during their 'journey' through the body. When this occurs, the bullet together with small fragments of bone are carried out through the exit wound, which will appear larger and more 'ragged' than that of the entry wound.

Entry wounds are easily recognisable by the discolouration of the surrounding skin. This discolouration is the result of residue emerging from the muzzle of the gun. In cases of very close or contact shootings, in which the muzzle is held against the victim's body, the skin surrounding the entry wound will be blackened and possibly pinkish due to the emission of carbon monoxide. In such cases, the entry wound will have splintered or have a star-shaped appearance. This is caused by the bullet emerging from the barrel as it will display some degree of 'wobbling' before it stabilises. This 'tail wag' tears the skin to produce the ragged edge. A shot fired from about one yard will display these characteristics but to a much lesser extent. The entry wound will be smaller, and the darkening or *tattooing* of the skin will be slighter. From a greater distance from the target, there will be little, or no 'tattooing' and the exit wound will appear roughly the same size as that of the entry wound.

The angle at which a bullet enters a body can be of evidential importance. It is possible to estimate the angle of entry by examining the blackening or 'tattooing' on the skin above the entry wound.

Characteristics Of A Shotgun Injury Relative To Distance

Contact	Few inches	One yard
Ragged Tear	1inch Irregular Hole	Single Hole
Burning	Burning	Soot
Soot	Soot	Tattooing
Tattooing	Tattooing	Carbon Monoxide

Two yards	Six yards	Twelve yards
Irregular Wound	Groups and	Uniform Pellet
Pellet Holes	Single Pellets	Spread over
Some Tattooing	Over 6-7 inches	12-14 inches
	diameter	diameter

Shot in its diffuse form, as fired from a distance has little penetrating power, and exit wounds are not a feature of shotgun injuries other than in the 'contact' situation. As the above chart indicates, the various effects characteristics of shotgun injuries diminish as the distance from muzzle to wound increases. The critical distance is at about 2 yards when at this distance tattooing is hardly visible. Any further than this distance and the shot begins to fan out, creating a pattern of entry in the clothing and on the skin of the victim. A simple rule of thumb is that the diameter of the shot pattern in centimetres is some 2.5 to 3.0 times the muzzle distance from the wound in metres (or the spread in inches is equivalent to the distance in yards). Fatal 12-bore shotgun injuries are unlikely at a range of over 20 yards. Gunshot wounds have characteristics that are significantly different from those of bullet wounds. In the case of contact or close-contact shots, these will result in the shot-pellets not spreading as they leave the shotgun barrel, the shots entering the body as a single mass. When fired from a greater distance, the pellets will fan out and cover a wider area of the body's surface, So, as a rough guide, the greater the area of shot spread, the further away the shotgun was fired. Often doubt exists as to whether a fatal shooting was a murder or a suicide. Clearly, if the distance from which a shot was fired is greater than the arm's length of the victim, then murder must be suspected.

[5] Poisoning (Toxicology)

It is a basic fact that any substance can, in theory, be poisonous, depending of course, on the circumstances of its use. The *toxicity* or poisonous effect of any substance depends on how much was ingested and over what period. In addition, the age and weight of an individual, together with their existing state of health, will determine whether or not a swallowed substance will cause death or injury. In forensic science, the usual questions that arise are; "Was the victim poisoned?", "What was the poison used?" and " Was it accidental, suicidal or murder?". The suspicion that someone may have been poisoned depends primarily on the general circumstances of each case. Once poisoning is suspected, then scientific techniques can be used.

Toxicology is the study of the effects of drugs and poisons on human beings, and the investigation of fatal intoxication for medico-legal investigation. The first step in any toxicological investigation is to obtain a sample from the deceased or, in the case of a non-fatal suspected poisoning, from the living victim. Samples taken from survivors are much easier to analyse because there is not the added problem of decomposition products being present in the samples, which would be the case with dead bodies. Before any analysis is undertaken, the samples are treated in such ways that the poison is extracted and purified, to exclude any other products being present.

As a means of identification of a particular poisonous substance, a technique known as *Chromatography* is used to separate the various compounds present in the sample. These different compounds will pass through an absorbent medium at 'different rates', which depend upon their chemical composition. In *gas chromatography,* the test substance is made volatile by heating the molecules from the various compounds which will then move through a long narrow tube of glass or steel, towards a detection monitor that 'recognises' the specific electrical impulses generated by each separate compound. A graphic recorder then produces a chart which plots the concentration of each compound which is displayed as a 'graph' showing a 'peak' against time. The time at which a compound appears on the graph is known as the 'retention time', and this retention time is specific to each compound. The subsequent height of each 'peak' on the graph reveals the quantity of poison compound present in each sample.

The problem of how the poison was administered is of crucial importance to a criminal investigation. It is relevant to the question of whether the case is one of accident, suicide or murder. Particular poisons are associated with particular forms of administration. For example, *cyanide* or *arsenic* are usually ingested through the mouth, while other substances such as *heroin* are most commonly injected directly into the bloodstream (intravenously). Other drugs such as *cocaine* and *nicotine* (in the form of 'snuff') are usually 'snorted' into the nose. They enter the body via the nasal membranes and blood vessels. Injecting such drugs as heroin directly into the bloodstream is an effective means of introducing the poison into the circulatory system.

Toxicologists use the term 'bioavailability' to describe the quantity of the drug taken that will cause a physiological effect on the body. In this way, the bioavailability of the drug *cannabis* is very low if swallowed because it is not easily absorbed during its passage through the digestive system. Conversely, the bioavailability of injected heroin is 100% effective, as are all substances taken intravenously.

As one would expect, the majority of poisons are administered by mouth. One major factor controlling the bioavailability of poisons taken orally is the metabolic action of the liver.

When drugs are absorbed in the intestine, they pass into the blood vessels that carry blood to the liver, where they are metabolised for energy. It is in the liver that many potentially poisonous compounds are deactivated. Although drugs may be absorbed in the digestive tract, their bioavailability is drastically reduced in the liver. Before the liver 'barrier' is reached, the poison's capability of being absorbed into the bloodstream must be prevented. Much depends on the chemical composition and structure of the substance. This bioavailability of a drug or poison can be an important legal concern. If the substance ingested was of such a dose and administered in a quantity that was unlikely to harm the person, these circumstances would be significant in a criminal trial. The forensic toxicologist can determine the type of poison administered and also its dosage. Metabolic activity results in the deactivation of poisons and their eventual excretion usually in the urine.

Heroin is one example of a substance that is

metabolised exceptionally rapidly. Toxicologists will, therefore, test for metabolites or excreted by-products. However, some compounds and their metabolites are retained in the body for a considerable period compared to most drugs. For example, cannabis metabolites are one example of compounds that can be retained in the body, sometimes for up to several weeks.

These toxicological facts and methods allow toxicologists to present vital information in cases of suspected murder or suicide. People committing suicide have been found to behave in a fairly predictable manner. In the case of suicide by poison, the 'victim' usually removes their spectacles before swallowing the fatal dose. Murderers may not be aware of this subtle fact and fail to remove their victim's spectacles. Although this reference to behaviour may not have a 'scientific' basis, it could suggest that a case may be one of murder and not suicide.

The techniques available to the forensic scientist are numerous, but it is the interpretation of the findings of any investigation that is of vital importance. For example, if the results of certain tests reveal that a particular poison was administered in a certain dose, what does this imply? It could be concluded that the kind and dosage of the drug were such as to cause death. This conclusion then raises a further question. What is the dosage that causes death? It is a known fact that some people can tolerate higher levels of certain poisons, depending upon their general medical condition, their size and weight. Other factors are relevant to the question of dosage. The concentration of a poison or a metabolite will also vary according to where in the circulatory system a blood sample was taken.

Because of the above, the interpretation of toxicological results must be made with extreme care. The toxicologist may need information about a victim's state of health before the death, or the nature of his or her last meal. If a dead body is infested with maggots, it is considered safer to conduct tests on the tissues of the maggots themselves, since such 'living' tissues would reveal more reliable results.

'*Toxicity Curves*' are graphs which plot the dosage against the effect of a particular drug and these have been stored on databases. In principle, such curves will rise at a shallow incline, then become much steeper before finally levelling off. At lower dosages where the incline is shallow, the poison may have little or no effect. At the lower end of the steep incline, symptoms of mild toxicity will appear. At the higher parts, symptoms of severe poisoning will appear. Finally, death will occur at the levelling-off phase.

Poisoning as a means of suicide appears to be much more common than it is for murder. However, it should also be remembered that those 'murders by poison' that have been detected are the only ones that have become public knowledge. The unsavoury fact remains that some murders involving poisons are discovered only by sheer good fortune. This does suggest that many more such murders are committed than is generally acknowledged.

Common Poisons

[1] Cyanide

Some of the most common poisons are termed *gaseous* or volatile poisons. What is generally termed 'cyanide' can be one of two chemical compounds; hydrocyanic or prussic acid (HCN) together with one of its salts, usually potassium cyanide (KCN). Hydrocyanic acid is the more fast-acting of the two. Acid and salt kill in the same manner - by blocking the mechanisms that enable the cells to receive oxygen from the blood. A consequence of this is the 'flushed' appearance of the victim, occurring because the haemoglobin in the red blood cells remains saturated with oxygen, and this forms unstable oxyhaemoglobin. Bright scarlet blotches appear on the skin of those who die from cyanide poisoning. There is also a distinctive smell of bitter almonds on the breath of the victim.

[2] Carbon Dioxide

Carbon dioxide (CO_2) is a natural gas present at a concentration of about 0.03% in the atmosphere. When it is concentrated in the lungs, this prevents expulsion from the body resulting in respiratory impairment. Concentration even as low as 3% in the atmosphere will result in symptoms of dizziness, headaches and general weakness. Concentrations of 25% and above are fatal. However, carbon monoxide (CO) is more deadly because it binds to haemoglobin to form the very stable compound *Carboxyhaemoglobin* and oxygen can no longer be carried by the blood. Death by CO poisoning is a common form of suicide, with the victim connecting a tube from a car exhaust to the interior of the car, death usually being very rapid. Of forensic significance is the fact that people who commit suicide in this way, take some trouble to be comfortable in the vehicle. It is not an impulsive action. These facts are useful in cases in which murder is made to appear like a suicide.

One of the post-mortem characteristics of death by CO poisoning is the development of bright red tinting on the skin, very similar to that of cyanide poisoning. However, there is no distinctive smell of bitter almonds in the mouth of the CO victim.

[3] Chloroform

Chloroform is a very well-known volatile substance although today it is not often used as a poison, being mainly restricted to medical settings. The most important medico-legal factor is that the point at which a victim relaxes under the effect of chloroform is very close to the point of death, which is due to paralysis of the heart muscles. An average fatal dose for an adult would be around 120 grams ingested.

[4] Stimulants, Excitants and Hallucinogenic Drugs

Of this group of systematic poisons, *amphetamines* are probably the best known. A typical example is known as 'speed', which provides the user with feelings of alertness, confidence and energy. However, the sudden withdrawal of this drug has the direct opposite effects; fatigue and depression, the typical 'highs' and 'lows' experienced by addicts. In some cases, this can ultimately result in heart attacks, strokes and death. Another 'popular' amphetamine is 'Ecstasy' or to give it its chemical name; 3, 4 - methylenedioxy-methamphetamine or MDM. It produces euphoria in the user which can develop into hallucinations. The main problem with this particular substance is that it is often mixed with other drugs of 'unknown' quantity.

The infamous LSD of the 1960s is an extremely dangerous and powerful hallucinogen, causing mental delusions such as paranoia, schizophrenia and psychological disorders. There are many poisons which are derived from plants. One example is 'atropine' or 'belladonna' which is derived from the plant *Deadly Nightshade*, with its dull purple flower and shiny blackberries.

Cocaine is another plant drug derived from the dried leaves of *Erythroxylin Coca,* a tropical plant grown in Africa, South America and South-east Asia. It is a powerful nerve stimulant, and overdoses can kill by overstimulation of the heart. It is a most dangerous drug usually taken as 'snuff'. Its most common usage today is as 'crack cocaine'. This is produced by heating cocaine with baking soda in water. The resulting mixture is dried and used for smoking. This form of the drug is more dangerous than straight cocaine.

Allied to the 'stimulant' drugs are 'convulsant' poisons of which *Strychnine* is one. It has an exceptionally bitter taste being extracted from the berries of the tree *Strychnos Nux Vomica,* or poison berry. It causes powerful convulsions and death follows from the paralysis of the 'medulla oblongata' in the brain.

[5] Tranquillisers

The analgesic, hypnotic and narcotic drugs, all of which are classed as 'tranquillisers' are among the most common poisons used in suicides today. This is because of the simple fact that most of them are readily available within the home. Paracetamol is one of the most common drugs at home, and people have attempted to commit suicide by taking massive overdoses. What is not generally known is that death is not very rapid with this drug. It can take up to two or three days of suffering before death due to chronic liver failure.

Among the hypnotic drugs, the *barbiturates*

are the most dangerous. They are often prescribed for tranquillising purposes, frequently taken with an alcoholic drink which enhances the effect of the drug, while significantly reducing the amount needed for a fatal dose. A dose of just 1 gram of some barbiturates can kill within minutes.

[6] Narcotic Drugs

The most common narcotic drug is *Opium* and its derivatives. By definition, a narcotic is a substance that dulls pain and reduces consciousness. Opium comprises the dried juice of the opium poppy (*Papaver Somniferum*) which is the substance that is smoked in a pipe. *Morphine* is a derivative of opium, and heroin or diamorphine is itself derived from morphine.

Other narcotic substances can be found in the opium resin extracted from the plant's seeds, such as *Codeine*. The only legitimate use of opium is in the form of extracted codeine and morphine, both of which are prescribed for use in a medical environment.

Laudanum, which is opium dissolved in alcohol, was widely used in Britain during the Victorian period.

The 'external' symptoms of opium poisoning are stupor leading to coma and heavy sweating. The pulse becomes slower, breathing also slows down, and the body becomes cold to the touch. The most distinctive symptom of opium poisoning is the contracting of the pupils into 'pin-points'. Since no two preparations of heroin will have the same percentage of impurities, the forensic toxicologist can determine whether two samples came from the same batch. Sometimes the difference between two samples may be evident from the difference in colour, although chemical and chromatographical tests can confirm this. Also, heroin derived from opium poppies grown in different regions of the world may have different chemical characteristics.

'Cutting agents' can also help to distinguish between batches. A 'cutting agent' is a substance like sugar or a barbiturate used to dilute the drug, or as a camouflage to obscure its purity.

The ultimate question as to what is the fatal dose of morphine or heroin is very difficult to answer definitively. The reason for this is that habitual 'users' may acquire a tolerance to the drug and can withstand much higher doses than those just starting on the drug. However, dosages of over 200 mg are lethal, although many people will succumb to much lower doses.

One of the most common and oldest drugs is *Cannabis,* the product of the plant *Cannabis Sativa.* It can be found as dried leaves, stems or flowers, and as a resin or oil. In terms of odour, it smells very much like spearmint.

Nicotine most commonly connected with cigarettes is not a widely used poison. However, fatalities do occur since the purified toxin is also used as insecticides and pesticides. Three or four drops of 'pure nicotine' will kill in a very short time once ingested.

[7] Poisons in General Use

There are other freely-available poisons which work owing to their general effect on body tissues as a whole. For example, strong acids and alkalis, as well as the salts of heavy metals, have a 'corrosive' or 'burning; action on body tissue. *Phenol* or carbolic acid is commonly used as in disinfectant and antiseptic preparations, mainly for domestic use. As a result, these are among the most used suicide poisons. Swallowing phenol results in a burning pain in the mouth and the digestive tract. Burn marks on the lips of suicides suggest that Phenol or one of its relatives has been used, together with the sweet smell of Phenol which is a good indicator.

Oxalic acid is found in many preparations used for cleaning metal and leather, particularly in brass polishing. A secondary effect of oxalic acid poisoning is its depression of blood calcium levels. The crystals of calcium oxalate are precipitated in the kidneys, a sure post-mortem indication of oxalic acid poisoning. The other main group of non-systematic poisons comprise those referred to as 'irritants'. These cause substantial irritation to the lining of the stomach. Although they are not fast-acting, they include one of the most commonly used poisons in history, the semi-metal *arsenic.*

Arsenic is obtained from its ore, *arsono pyrite,* which is a greyish-white mineral containing iron and sulphur, together with arsenic itself. The white oxide is extracted by placing the ore in a container and heating it to a high temperature. When the vapour it produces condenses on the walls of the container, traces of arsenic are found. Symptoms of arsenic poisoning are vomiting, followed by immense stomach pains, diarrhoea, cramps, loss of weight, constriction of the throat and 'melanosis', darkening of the skin. These are the symptoms of chronic poisoning, but in acute cases in which a large dose is ingested, the pulse grows weak and muscular convulsions appear before death.

Arsenic was the first poison for which a diagnostic test was devised. In 1836, James Marsh published a paper which appeared in the *Edinburgh New Philosophical Journal.* This described his method for converting traces of arsenic into 'arsine' gas from which very minute amounts of arsenic can be identified.

The general principles of the Marsh Test are still followed by forensic scientists today. The test involves adding to the suspect fluid, and a small quantity of sulphuric acid to a piece of zinc. The reaction of the zinc and sulphuric acid will produce only hydrogen. However, if arsenic is present in the solution, 'arsine' will be given off. This gas can be determined by igniting it, then holding a piece of glass above the flame. If arsenic is present in the gas, it will be deposited on the glass.

One significant attribution of arsenic is that it will remain 'detectable' in the body long after death. This is because much of it is excreted into many parts of the body, including the hair and fingernails. An example of this particular phenomenon was seen when Emperor Napoleon's body was exhumed from its grave on the island of St Helena for reburial in France. The body was found to be almost uncorrupted. Large amounts of arsenic were found in his hair. This led to the suggestion that he had been deliberately poisoned. This was never proven, but the body's preserved state was clearly down to the presence of arsenic. Later tests conducted on Napoleon's hair concluded that the arsenic was not a contaminant from the soil in the grave, but an internal compound of the hair itself. As would be expected, the mystery of Napoleon's death abounds with conspiracy theories.

Chapter Five: A Case Of Identity

The previous chapters have been concerned with the "Where?" the "When?" and the "How?" of a criminal investigation. We now turn our attention to the "Who?" or how to identify the perpetrator of a crime.

Several references have been made to Locard's Principle as the basic tenet of forensic science. However, there is another equally important principle to consider, which is that of *Individuality*. This principle states that no two objects are identical, and consequently, no two people, documents or fingerprints are identical. As a result, forensic techniques have been developed that enable us to distinguish between things and persons.

The first real attempt to identify people on a scientific basis was during the second half of the nineteenth century. Alphonse Bertillon, a French scientist, devised a system known as *Anthropometry*. This involved taking measurements of key facial and body features. However, it proved to be of limited success because it was impossible to predict the probability of two individuals having the same set of measurements. Also, Bertillon was taking these measurements from known criminals and not including the general population.

However, Bertillon is perhaps better known for another technique he devised known as *portrait-parle*, or " a speaking portrait". This system compared various forms of facial features which could be built up to form a picture or 'portrait'. Its practical use was to enable French police officers to describe a wanted suspect in a manner that would allow others to form an image of the person being sought. It was not until the period of the Second

World War that real advances were made in identification techniques.

Identikit was a method invented by American Hugh McDonald. This system consisted of a series of transparencies displaying various forms of facial features which could be superimposed on one another, to provide a facial representation. It was possible to vary each feature according to witness statements, such as eye-forms, chin and nasal features. The success of '*Identikit*' lay in its ability to produce a near accurate description of an offender.

Further developments followed, one in Britain with a novel technique called *Photo FIT*, the FIT being an abbreviation for 'Facial Identification Technique'. In many ways, it is very similar to Identikit. However, instead of using transparencies, it uses actual photographs of facial features which total almost 100 mouth forms and 80 nose forms. It is possible to create multiple different facial compositions using PhotoFIT. With the application of computer software programmes today, it is now possible to reconstruct faces in various dimensions and colours.

[1] Fingerprints

Fingerprint analysis is regarded as the 'classic' tool of crime detection. Fingerprints compare numerous 'ridges' arranged in concentric circles. Some of these ridges end suddenly while others end in forks. The actual number of permutations is infinite, hence the assertion that no two individuals have identical fingerprints. It is the various features of a fingerprint, together with their relative positions on the print that enable the fingerprint examiner to identify a particular set as belonging to a specific individual.

In the UK, the usual method adopted is to match 16 points of similarity on the print of a suspect with the print retrieved from a crime scene. If they match exactly, then a positive identification can be made. In practice, an examiner will study the prints as a whole before making any comparison between equivalent parts of the prints to see whether they match. Having established that the two prints came from the same individual, a list will be compiled of the 16 points before a formal report is submitted.

An examination of fingerprints is usually carried out at the crime scene. There are various ways in which a print can be enhanced or 'lifted' to use police jargon.

Readers familiar with popular TV crime dramas such as "*CSI*" and "*Silent Witness*" will have noted the use of carbon or aluminium powders used for enhancing fingerprints for photographing before their 'lifting'. Lifting is carried out by placing low-adhesive tape on the enhanced print and carefully removing it. This is then stuck down on a piece of white card on which details of the particular case are recorded.

In the UK and many other countries, the taking of fingerprints is now totally computerised. Previously, the standard procedure was to coat the fingers of a suspect with ink and impression were taken on a standard form. The suspect's prints are then scanned into a database for a possible match.

Most of the 43 police forces in the UK use the computer system NAFIS (National Automated Fingerprint Intelligence System). The computer uses a special algorithm to select several characteristics that can determine the closest matches between a suspect's fingerprint held in the database and that recovered from a crime scene. However, the fingerprint examiner will also carry out a comparison using a photograph of the crime scene mark, together with the one from the suspect's fingerprints, which will be viewed side by side on a variation of the 'Comparison Microscope'.

[2] Forensic Anthropology

Forensic Anthropology is the examination of human skeletal remains to determine the identity of an individual skeleton. Physical anthropologists have developed methods to evaluate bones that have been discovered.

When the remains of an unknown person are discovered, attempts are first made to establish what kind of person they were. Forensic anthropology aims to determine the sex, age, stature and conditions of bones within a legal context. There are fundamental questions which arise; are they male or female, young or old, black or white? When a physical description of the person is made, then the investigation will focus on a specific identity, hopefully to answer the question, "Who was he or she?"

Through established methods, a forensic anthropologist can assist a criminal investigation be establishing a profile of the unidentified remains. This profile will include such details as sex, age, ethnicity, stature, length of time since death, and the evidence of any trauma revealed by analysis of the bones.

The stages of growth and development in bones and teeth provide valuable information about whether the remains represent a child or an adult. The shape of pelvic bones provides the best evidence for the sex of the person. Abnormal changes in the shape, size and density of bones can indicate disease and trauma.

Establishing the sex of skeletal remains is

usually a routine matter unless the person was a very young child or youth in the process of developing into adulthood when sexual differences are not always apparent. In adults, various bones can indicate the sex of the remains. The most obvious is the pelvic girdle, which has a very characteristic form in adult males and females, which relate to the child-bearing ability of the female.

Bones marked by perimortem injuries (those inflicted around the time of death) such as unhealed fractures, bullet holes or cuts, can reflect the cause of death. Skull shape and dental traits differ in individuals of diverse ancestry. Even certain activities, diet and ways of life, can be revealed in the bones and teeth.

Forensic anthropologists employ a variety of techniques to analyse human remains and record their observations. For example, recovered bones are usually photographed and X-rayed. Some remains may even undergo CT scanning or be examined with high-powered microscopes. Today, DNA analysis may also be used to help establish identity. However, mitochondrial DNA in bones and teeth can be valuable in confirming relationships of skeletal remains with possible living descendants.

Other chemical analyses, such as those involving isotopes, can provide valuable information relating to the age of the bones, an individual's diet and even country of origin. All the data collected from various sources is studied and combined to form a profile of the deceased individual. In a criminal case today, photographs of the skull may be superimposed on those of missing persons to identify consistencies between the bones and flashed forms of the skull. Even in those cases where no photographs are available, the face can be reconstructed based on the underlying bone structure and known standards for facial tissue thickness.

Estimating an individual's age at death is easier in young people than adults because of the many changes that occur in the morphology and anatomy of children. When bones fuse or when teeth erupt, these factors can be used with a reasonable degree of accuracy to determine age. Conversely, in adults, these changes do not occur, so that age determination is more difficult to establish.

The 'height' of an individual during life is relatively easy to determine, provided that a complete skeleton is available for analysis. Measurement of the bones, together with the addition of a 'correction factor' to adjust for the absence of soft tissues, will determine the 'stature' of the individual pretty accurately.

Problems do arise when the skeleton recovered is incomplete. However, the surviving individual bones will provide some indication of the 'height', but the reliability of that information varies from one bone to another. The bones of the lower limbs such as the femur, tibia and fibula, are better guides to height than the upper limbs.

The skeletons of young people present some difficulty if only because different children grow at diffcrent rates, so there is no uniform consistency. To determine the stature of a child from its skeletal remains, it would be necessary to know both the age and the sex beforehand. Another problem with determining stature from skeletal remains is that the base-line data collected from living people is often incomplete.

One of the most problematic questions is that of race or ethnic origin. The main difficulty here is that race is not always clearly defined and can vary

75

from person to person. Also, there is much more intermarriage between different racial groups today than in the past, which can add further confusion.

However, certain generalisations can be made about the differences in the morphology of the 'skull' between Europeans and black Africans. For example, the erosion of teeth may suggest a particular type of diet which included gritty rough food.

Various diseases present in life may leave their mark on limbs of the skeleton, and their presence adds another aspect of the person. For example, degenerative joint diseases such as arthritis may leave the mark as massive new bone formation. Once a 'generic' description of a person has been established the question of specific identification can then be attempted. The teeth are particularly useful in this respect because they vary considerably between individuals. Also, records of most people are held by dentists, usually as computer data. This data is a useful reference to check for identification of an unknown individual.

[3] Cranio- Facial Reconstruction

Another technique used for identifying individuals where only skeletal remains are available is that of facial reconstruction. This technique was pioneered by a Swiss anatomist, William His. He worked from the bone structure of the face to reconstruct the facial appearance of people as they had been in life. It is on record that he was presented with a skull supposedly that of the famous German composer Johann Sebastian Bach. His reconstruction was later compared with available portraits of the composer painted during Bach's lifetime. The likeness produced was so realistic that the skull from which he had worked was officially proclaimed to be that of Bach. The technique was further developed by Professor Grigoriev, a professor of forensic medicine in Moscow around 1920. Grigoriev, together with his assistant, Mikhail Gerasimov studied the heads of corpses collected for anatomy classes. The men collected data relating to the thickness of the face's soft tissues on the bony framework of the skull. In 1925, Gerasimov moved from Moscow to Siberia, having been appointed head of the department of archaeology at the city museum in Irkutsk. His work involved recreating the faces of the earliest men from fossils discovered in the Siberian tundra.

One such commission was to reconstruct the face of Mongol conqueror Tamerlane (1336-1405) from the skull found in his tomb. In the UK, the technique was first used by Dr Richard Neave, a medical illustrator in the Department of Anatomy at Manchester University Medical School. Initially, it was applied to provide recognisable faces of historical characters such as Philip II of Macedon, father of Alexander the Great. However, in 1987 the most horrific fire broke out in the subway of King's Cross Station in London in which 32 people lost their lives. The Metropolitan Police contacted Dr Neave to produce a likeness of the one victim of the fire who remained unidentified. He produced a likeness of the victim's face from the recovered skull and photographs of the reconstruction were circulated in the press. The resulted in the identity of this final victim being made by a relative.

The process of reconstructing is begun by making a cast of the skull of the individual. A series of holes are then drilled into the cast at specific anatomical reference points. A wooden rod is then inserted into each of the holes and secured so that it protrudes only to a depth that is consistent with the universally-accepted data for the depth of soft-tissue layers at each point. The eye sockets are filled with plastic 'eye-balls', and the muscular structure of the face is then built up by applying layers of modelling clay, to the surface of the skull until each of the wooden rods is just covered. The modelling begins with the neck and jaw before continuing upward to the cheeks and eyes. The 'tissues' laid over the forehead, the sides, and top of the head are thinner than those covering the lower parts of the face where the bones lie further below the skin surface. The contours of the cheeks and jaws are then smoothed, together with the whole surface of the clay to represent human skin. This is usually followed with more superficial touches which are added to give the model a more life-like appearance. However, these extra 'touches' are not wholly reliable representations since the skeleton provides little constructive information on such features as the shape of the nose, eyebrows or style of hair. Such features are usually left to the 'artistic' discretion of the individual illustrator. Despite this very minor 'exception', many reconstructions have been found to resemble the subject's genuine appearance closely.

With the widespread development of computer programmes today in most areas of science, facial reconstruction is no exception. Consequently, most current craniofacial reconstruction is now performed using digital imaging. However, the general principles of reconstruction are the same; the only difference being the speed in which the process can be completed. Digital reconstruction commences by producing a digital image of a skull using a laser scanner. This then creates a 'virtual' model of the skull. However, having the actual skull available is the most accurate since there are many surface details on the bone, which can provide clues to the facial appearance of the individual. Once the skull has been scanned, it is then possible to view and interact with the 3D 'virtual' skull. The face can be sculptured onto it without risking any damage to the 'original' skull. Employing this technique also makes the anatomical re-assembling of broken or fragmented skulls much easier. The overall shape of a human face falls within the range between two extremes; *Brachycephaly* which means wide and short, and *Dolichocephaly* meaning narrow and long.

Facial reconstruction is a mixture of 'objective' science and 'subjective anatomical interpretation. While it remains a much-disputed area of forensic anthropology, it has nevertheless been repeatedly successful in cases of forensic identification of the dead. Facial reconstruction is not only utilised in forensic human identification for 'unknown' individuals, but also in archaeological and historical investigations.

An excellent example of this was the BBC programme *"Meet the Ancestors"* shown on TV some years ago. Once a facial reconstruction has been created, there are numerous avenues open to the police to advertise and gain maximum public response. Ideally, this would be 'intelligence' led dependent upon the individual circumstances of each case.

For example, if it was believed that the person lived in the specific locality where the remains were discovered, use could be made of local media and distribution of posters. From a police intelligence perspective, the *National Missing Persons Unit* in the UK hold a database of all reported missing persons which will be searched as an initial inquiry. For a large inquiry, the police would use the HOLMES database (Home Office Large Major Enquiry System). On this system, there are recorded all possible leads and links to aid identification of individuals.

The easiest way to decide what is and what is not important in identifying persons is to exclude people who it cannot be. There are various ways of doing this, the most common method being DNA profiling which can be the quickest and most conclusive tool to exclude or include people. If no DNA is available, other methods can be applied.

Forensic Odontology allows for teeth comparisons to be made with dental records. In this way, the dentist can match the teeth of the victim to any records held on dental databases.

Also, medical implants found on skeletal remains, such as a hip replacement, will have a material serial number which can be traced to medical and manufacturer's records.

If, despite maximum publicity by the police, a significant response is not forthcoming, this would then indicate that the person may not be local, but perhaps a visitor or someone who worked or studied in the area of discovery on a temporary basis. Further searches can then be made involving INTERPOL, the 'International Police Organisation' to which most world-wide countries contribute, who have databases of wanted and missing persons.

[4] DNA Fingerprinting

DNA fingerprinting is now seen as being the most powerful and reliable tool in the forensic scientist's armoury. However, it is a much-misunderstood technique.

What is DNA? It is the genetic material of the cell, and it largely determines our physical characteristics. The abbreviation is a shorthand form of *deoxyribonucleic acid,* which is present in the cell nucleus and extra-nuclear organelles of the cell, known as *mitochondria.* We inherit half of our nuclear DNA from our fathers and half from our mothers. However, we receive all our mitochondrial DNA or (mtDNA) from our mothers.

Consequently, nuclear DNA provides information about our paternal and maternal relations, while (mtDNA) provides information only on our 'maternal' descent.

The basic principle is that specific stretches of DNA are believed to be unique to an individual. Consequently, no other individual will have the same DNA along those stretches, unless they were identical twins of the individual. When a sample of tissue, blood, semen or skin is found at a crime scene, it can be recovered and used as a source of DNA. Once the DNA is extracted from the sample, it is cut into little pieces by certain enzymes which act as chemical 'scissors'. This mixture of DNA pieces is placed on a gel plate, through which an electric current is passed. The different pieces will separate from each other as they move along the gel, the larger ones moving faster and further than the smaller ones.

This process remains invisible to the human eye, so radioactive labelled pieces of DNA are added which adhere to the pieces already separated. The radioactivity makes these pieces visible when an X-ray film of the gel is produced. It is in this way that a picture or print of the DNA can be made and compared with a similar print of the DNA taken from a suspect. If the samples match precisely, one then has a 'positive' identification. The DNA profile or 'fingerprint' is usually represented as a series of 'bands' very like 'bar-codes' found on supermarket products.

DNA fingerprinting has had many notable successes. Its failures, however, have not always received similar publicity. DNA fingerprinting is of no practical use unless you have some idea as to where the victim or the offender to a crime may have been at the material time. No evidence is 'infallible' - not even DNA. Arriving at the truth in a forensic investigation is a case of attacking one perceived problem from many different angles. If all the evidence strands support the emerging theory, there is then a good reason to believe that the truth has been achieved.

Contrary to widespread beliefs, science is an endeavour that is mainly concerned with 'probabilities' and not certainties. Scientists in general and forensic scientists in particular, do not 'know' things in a different kind of way than other people do; they can only suggest a 'probability' for something happening.

DNA results are no exception to this rule because they are no more 'scientific' or 'true' than the rest of the evidence presented in a criminal case. They are as much subject to the laws of probability as anything else. In science, one accepts an idea, concept or hypothesis, as long as there is no evidence to contradict it. Due to its many impressive results, and its assumed powerful scientific base, DNA evidence has acquired a mantle of <u>invincibility</u> that cannot and should not be accorded to any scientific discipline. However, such is the strength of belief in DNA evidence, that its results often appear to make people, including some scientists, override logic. It is dangerous to give a particular scientific technique an aura of infallibility because this tends to close the mind against other valid evidence. Unfortunately, many people have a strong attachment to particular lines of forensic evidence based mainly on current popular techniques. Therein lies the danger. The longer the chain of transference of DNA from primary contact, through secondary contacts onwards, the smaller the amount is transferred. The presence of a person's DNA at a particular scene may have significance, but, equally, it may not.

A further complication arises once the crime scene is investigated. All the individuals present at the scene bring with them a potential array of DNA (both their own and other people's which have been picked up accidentally). This comes with their bodies, clothes and the tools they use.

This transference raises a further question. Is the 'scene of crime kit' DNA free? Short of eliminating DNA evidence totally, the best one can do is to ensure that 'contamination' is reduced to a minimum.

On leaving the crime scene, collected samples have to be transported and stored at the laboratory. Then it is unpacked and examined, the DNA extracted, amplified and analysed. At each of these stages, the risk of contamination must be considered. Assuming that a reliable match is achieved on DNA analysis, and given the enhanced specificity of the test, there is the question relating to the chance that it may have come from someone else, unrelated to the 'matched' person. This is probably expressed today in millions.

Let us suppose that there has been a murder, and your DNA is found on the murder weapon. Let us further suppose that this match is calculated to have a probability of one in a million out of a total population of say fifty million. The probability that your DNA would match that of the murderer is one in a million. Or is it? The probability of it matching you is one in a million if you are a randomly selected person. However, this implies that there are another forty-nine people who also match the DNA. So the probability that you committed the murder is only 2%. The following media extracts highlight the need for 'caution' in DNA evidence in criminal trials.

Juries Are Misled Over DNA Evidence: Experts Dispute Accuracy Of Test

"Forensic experts have seriously misled juries over the strengths of genetic fingerprint evidence, two leading mathematicians suggest today. In an article in this week's issue of the science journal *Nature,* the pair set out detailed criticisms of the way forensic experts present what appear to be huge odds against wrongful identification by the fingerprint technique. David Balding and Peter Donnelly of Queen Mary and Westfield Colleges of London University say analysis of DNA, which carries the unique genetic material that makes an individual, is valuable in establishing innocence but should not be used as the 'sole basis' for conviction. The costs of previous misunderstandings in unsafe convictions are impossible to assess. The two mathematicians say that DNA profiles can, in the absence of other evidence, leave a realistic 'chance' that at least one other person than the suspect could be the criminal. DNA fingerprinting relies on the fact that apart from identical twins, no two people have the same DNA genetic code in their cells. The technique uses 'probes' to pick out key features of the code in samples from scenes of crime. If these features match those in the DNA fingerprint from a suspect, there is strong evidence that the samples came from that person. Forensic scientists often describe to juries the extremely 'small' probabilities of anyone but the suspect producing so strong a match with DNA taken from samples, one in several million is not an uncommon figure.

Instead of emphasising the slim chance of a DNA match being produced by an innocent person, courts should consider the probability of a person being innocent in spite of their having produced a match. To do this, the court should weigh up all other evidence of innocence. "I don't want to rule out the use of DNA fingerprinting, but would like to see the prosecution being more careful in explaining to juries how they should interpret DNA evidence", Professor Balding said yesterday. Professor Donnelly's fresh approach to the value of DNA fingerprinting, help convince the Court of Appeal last year to question the conviction of Andrew Dean for rape, the first UK challenge. The court ordered a retrial. At Mr Dean's original trial in 1990, it was claimed that the probability of a match was one in 700,000. At the retrial in 1993, a second opinion of this probability reduced it to 1 in 33."

Source: *The Independent,* 24 March, 1994: Susan Walls, Science Correspondent.

'DNA Evidence Doesn't Give A 'Yes / No Answer And Can Only Be Expressed In Terms Of A Probability' Say Forensic Scientists'

"The power of DNA to convict and exonerate is not 'infallible' according to a leading group of forensic scientists. While forensic evidence has given prosecutors and police a vital tool in their investigations and in court, researchers argue that we should acknowledge that the science is not foolproof and can rarely stand alone. The DNA evidence will not give a "Yes" or "No" answer, it can only be expressed in terms of 'probability.' We all enjoy a good crime drama and although we understand the difference between fiction and reality, the distinction can often be blurred by overdramatised press reports of real cases" says Denise Syndercombe Court, a reader in forensic genetics at King's College, London. " As a result, most people have unrealistic perceptions of the meaning of scientific evidence, especially when it comes to DNA, which can lead to miscarriages of justice" One such miscarriage of justice involved Adam Scott, who was charge with raping a woman in a town he claimed he had never visited in his life. In October 2011, DNA evidence was used to arrest the teenager from Plymouth for an alleged sexual assault that had taken place 200 miles away in Manchester. A forensic scientist claimed that the evidence was strong, despite the fact that a DNA profile on its own cannot provide any information about the body fluid it came from or lead to the inference that sexual intercourse took place. Mobile phone records eventually proved that Mr Scott had been in his home town at the time of the alleged assault. After five months in custody, he was released. Mr Scott had been the unfortunate victim of laboratory cross-contamination. Months earlier he had been involved in a 'spitting' incident in Exeter after which the police took a swab of his saliva. Scientists placed the swab in a tray at the LGC Forensic Laboratory, which was then re-used for the swab taken from the rape victim in Manchester. The real perpetrator has never been found."
Source: www.thejusticegap.com /2017/dna evidence

In most court cases where DNA evidence is introduced, a questioned sample, i.e. one whose origin is unknown yields a DNA profile that matches that of the suspect. The question then arises that this match might not be due to the suspect being the originator of the sample, but that the suspect possesses the same profile of that of the questioned sample by 'chance'. It is the forensic expert witness's responsibility to guide the court as to the likelihood and credibility of the match. The more frequent the profile is, the more 'credible' a coincidental match. One of the most challenging circumstances is where a piece of biological evidence is composed of a mixture of body fluids from different people. Where there are only two contributors, and with one having a more significant proportion of the DNA than the other, then it may be easy to allocate the higher match to the dominant contributor. I leave the final word on the subject of DNA profiling to the eminent British defence barrister Michael Mansfield QC:

"DNA is undoubtedly a remarkable discovery, but like any scientific advance, it should be treated with respect and we should all be vigilant about its limitations."

Source: Michael Mansfield: Memoirs of a Radical Lawyer, (Bloomsbury Publications Plc, London, (2009), p.201.

Chapter Six: Blood Pattern Analysis

Blood Pattern Analysis (or BPA) is the term most commonly used to describe the examination, identification and interpretation of patterns of blood-staining in relation to the action which caused them. BPA has played a vital role at the scenes of violent crime, where it forms an integral component of the reconstruction of the event. BPA is now applied regularly in the forensic laboratory to the 'distribution' of blood on such items as clothing and weapons recovered from crime scenes. By its very nature, the identification of bloodstain patterns is 'subjective', but it is underpinned by sound scientific principles.

Every bloodstain pattern is unique, but by applying these principles, the identification and interpretation of patterns can be made 'objective' so to be used in legal contexts. BPA may assist a criminal investigation at crime scenes where assaults are known to have occurred. It may also be possible to establish the relative positions of both the assailant(s) and victim(s), and the possible chains or sequences of events that have taken place. The presence of 'spattered clotted blood' provides a good indication of an 'interrupted' or prolonged assault having taken place.

Recognising staining patterns greatly increases the chances of locating blood from different sources, and this determines the samples that are taken for DNA profiling. It may also be possible to assess the degree to which an assailant would have become bloodstained during the process of carrying out the assault. Analysis of bloodstain patterns will usually be limited to addressing such issues as whether the staining resulted from an accident or a crime, and if the volume of blood can be estimated, whether the person who shed the blood is likely to be dead or still alive. In situations where a defendant or a suspect offers an explanation of the events that caused the bloodshed, these present the opportunity to test those hypotheses that relate specifically to the concerns of both the prosecution and defence in a case. What follows is a brief outline of the basics of BPA and how it is used in the investigation of violent crime. It is only by understanding the dynamics of the various actions that cause blood-stain patterns that the scientist can provide reasoned answers to questions asked by criminal investigators and courts of law. There are six categories of blood-stain patterns which will now be considered.

[1] Single Drops

This category concerns blood drops falling vertically under the force of gravity. A free-falling drop of blood is spherical, and its volume is determined by the shape and size of the surface on which it lands. If this is a large surface, then the drops will tend to be larger. However, if the dropping surface is very small, then no drops can form.

When a drop of blood falls onto a smooth surface, the stain will be circular, but those falling on to rough surfaces will be 'approximately' circular but with irregular edges. The size and shape of the stain produced by a drop of blood falling under gravity perpendicular on to a target surface will depend on these three variables.

Firstly, the greater the volume of the drop, the larger the stain for the same dropping height and target surface.

Secondly, the dropping height is in proportion to the size of the stain.

Finally, non-absorbent surfaces will result in the formation of larger stains because the entire volume of the drop will spread over the surface. On absorbent surfaces, the stains will appear smaller because a proportion of the blood is absorbed within the target surface.

Secondary spatter consists of small droplets of uniform size about 1-2mm in diameter. These drops are projected at low velocity; the distance travelled depending upon the volume of blood involved, the dropping height and the nature of the target surface. Often when an injured person drips blood on to the ground, secondary spatter will impact on the footwear and lower clothing of a person nearby in the form of small bloodstains. If DNA testing reveals this to match the injured person, then the presence of this secondary spatter is strong evidence that the two people were close together when the bleeding occurred, within 1 metre.

[2] Impact Spatter

This is the most common type of pattern seen in blood pattern analysis. It can result from a wide range of actions, kicking, stamping, beating, punching and shooting. The cause of impact spatter is a force impacting directly into wet blood which breaks up the blood into small droplets of varying volume. These droplets are dispersed radially from the impact site, having various trajectories and velocities. As a general rule, the greater the force applied, the smaller the average size of the droplets. The 'force' is that which is applied at the site of the impact. Many variables will affect the distance, direction and quantity of blood spattered by an impact.

Variables include the amount of wet blood at the impact site, the position of the impact site relative to the attacker, the shape and size of the weapon used in the attack, and the speed and angle of the weapon at the moment of impact. Detailed examination of patterns can provide valuable information to a criminal investigation. Recognising impact spatter allows the identification of the site of attack, and determines the relative positions of objects and people at the crime scene. The patterns may also offer information on the nature of the impact that caused the spatter. Most importantly, they can give an indication of the likelihood of blood staining being present on the assailant or others present at the scene, helping to determine the significance of bloodstains found on a suspect's clothing.

Examples of 'Impact Spatter'

In cases where an assailant bludgeons his victim with a <u>club hammer,</u> this will usually involve numerous blows, and considerable spatter will have been directed <u>back</u> towards the assailant. However, it is still possible for the majority of spatter from such a beating to be directed forwards or to the sides away from the assailant. In situations where there have been many blows, it is highly likely that the assailant will be blood- stained to some extent. Yet with a single or just a few blows, it may be that no blood is directed towards the assailant. When kicking or stamping of a victim is involved, a wide range of patterns may be seen, typically on footwear and trousers. Forceful contact with a shoe would force blood into the crevices around its seams. Stamping with the heel of the shoe will produce spatter that travels up inside the lower part of the trouser leg. <u>Punching</u> into wet blood will cause impact spatter that may be visible around the cuff and on the inside of the shirt.

It should be noted that a bleeding nose may produce a significant amount of blood loss, but afterwards, there may be no visible injury.

With an assault by stabbing, a single stab to the body rarely causes blood to be transferred to the assailant. Most of the bleeding will be 'internal' or absorbed by the victim's clothing. However, in the case of contact with the victim, or if several stabbings occur, there will then be a transfer of blood.

When a person is shot in the head at close range, the bloodstain patterns are affected by several factors, including the injury site, type and calibre of weapon, and distance between muzzle and skin.

A contact or near-contact injury from a shotgun will probably result in an extensive spattering of blood, tissue and bone fragments. Most of this will travel away from the victim in the general direction of the initial shot, but away from the person firing the weapon. This is usually referred to as Forward Spatter, because it is directed away from the assailant, meaning that the shooter may receive little or no blood on their clothing. A contact or near-contact injury to the head from a shotgun may also produce an aerosol of blood droplets that travel back towards the person firing the weapon. This is referred to as Back Spatter. However, these 'mist-like' blood droplets are unlikely to travel more than about 1 metre from the injury site and are not easily recognised on clothing.

Determining the Origin of Impact Spatter

Locating the position from which an 'impact' spatter originated is an essential element in reconstructing a crime scene. For many years, a technique known as stringing has been used, which is based on trigonometry. For example, for an impact spatter onto a horizontal surface, a straight line is drawn through the length of several bloodstains. Where these lines intersect is termed the Area of Convergence. The actual impact site will be somewhere on a vertical above the point of convergence.

In the 1980s, the Royal Canadian Mounted Police developed two computer programmes called *Backtrack* and *Images* to determine the area of convergence. A number of selected stains are photographed using a digital camera, then the *'Images'* programme calculates the angle at which the stains landed on the surface. The data and patterns are processed by *Backtrack* to produce a graphical representation of the 'area of origin'.

[3] Cast-Off

This term is applied to blood thrown from the surface of a moving object either by the action of centrifugal force (Swing Cast-Off) or by the object being brought to an abrupt halt (Cessation Cast-Off).

Swing Cast-Off

This is most often associated with the swinging of a weapon. Centrifugal force will cause wet-blood on the surface of the weapon, to run towards its far end, allowing it to pool at one or more sites, depending on the shape of the weapon or object. The size of the droplets cast off from a swinging weapon will depend on the shape of the object, the nature of its surface, the velocity with which it is swung and the amount of blood on the object.

Pronounced Cast-Off

This staining appears some distance away from the site of attack (often on ceilings) and is only

seen with the use of long, light, weapons. Short and
heavy weapons tend to be swung more slowly and in
shorter arches, using the weapon to cause damage,
and are less likely to produce cast-off. As more force
can be applied on the 'forward swing' of a weapon,
than its back swing, it is easier to generate cast-off
when a weapon is swung in a forward direction.

Cessation Cast-Off
       This term is applied to situations where the
swing of a weapon or object is abruptly stopped,
which causes rapid deceleration together with a large
amount of cast-off. During the swing phase, blood
will tend to form into runs towards the distal end of
the weapon.

[4] Arterial Damage Stains

       Most of the body's arteries are well-protected
against damage during normal activities. However, in
violent assaults and other incidents, they can become
damaged by sharp-edged instruments or by blunt
instrument trauma. The arteries most commonly
damaged in assaults are:

1. Temporal - Found at both sides of the forehead.
2. Carotid - Found at both sides of the neck.
3. Radial - Found near the surface of the wrist.
4. Aorta - The main vessel leading from the heart,
located deep in the chest cavity.
5. Femoral - Located in the thigh, running from the
groin to the knee.
6. Brachial - Located in the inner side of the upper
arm.

       When an artery is damaged, the blood is
emitted in a <u>column</u> which then breaks up into

individual droplets of approximately equal size. Blood leaves the artery in a series of <u>spurts</u> that correspond to the beating of the heart. If the injured person is moving, it can result in "U" or "W" shaped patterns. Arterial <u>gush</u> results from a stream of blood hitting a surface, producing a large stain. 'Arterial rain' is the term used to describe blood that has spurted into the air, then fallen to the ground under gravity.

[5] Contact Stains

This category includes stains whose appearance is due to direct contact between an object wet with blood and another surface. During the examination of a blood-stained crime scene or blood-stained clothing, it is probable that any number of stains will be found that have no clearly defined shape. Contact stains are of particular interest if there is information available about the bloodied object that left the patterns. This would be the case with a fingerprint, shoe-mark or weapon impression.

The Evaluation of Bloodstain Pattern Evidence

Rapid developments in DNA technology have allowed precise discrimination between individuals. If a blood stain's DNA profile matches an individual, the likelihood of it being a 'random' match is in the order of one per 'billion'. The strength of this blood evidence means that both suspects and defendants are obliged to explain how such blood came to be on their clothing.

For example, where an individual is suspected of assault by kicking, it is not uncommon to find the victim's blood on their shoes. The suspect may explain by admitting they were present at the scene but to administer first aid to the victim.

The question then arises of how do courts assess the validity of such an explanation when the prosecution suggests that the blood got on the defendant's shoes because it was he who did the kicking.

In such a case, it is no longer necessary just to show that the blood on the defendant's shoes matched that of the victim. The forensic scientist is required to evaluate the appearance and distribution of the blood staining. How is this evaluation carried out?

Evidence is evaluated in the light of other relevant information in the case. It is also necessary to consider the prosecution and defence propositions. It is also necessary to consider such questions as "What is the probability of the evidence if the prosecution's proposition is true, compared to that of the defence?" The ratio of these probabilities is known as the Likelihood Ratio.

If we refer to our hypothetical case of the alleged kicking, the prosecution proposes that the defendant kicked the victim, and the defence proposes that the defendant did not kick the victim, but instead offered fist aid. What would be our expectations if either the prosecution or the defence is correct?

Experiments have been conducted with people wearing different types of footwear, who have simulated violent kicking attacks, on to a bloody surface. Various characteristic features of the bloodstains are regularly seen, indicative of forceful contact. Included here is the presence of contact staining in the crevices of the shoe and directional spattered blood associated with contact stains. Consequently, if the suspect has this type of staining on his shoes, this evidence will support the prosecution's proposition. However, what might be expected if as the defence maintains, the defendant was just administering first aid?

Other experiments have shown that such 'incidental' contact will indeed produce contact bloodstains. However, these would not be of the type indicating that 'any force' had been used and there would be no associated spatter. This pattern of staining on the shoes then supports the defence proposition. The ability of forensic scientists to assess and interpret evidence is central to the development of many areas of forensic science.

When the presence of blood is suspected, some preliminary tests are carried out as a matter of routine.

One of the most common of these is the *Phenolphthalein or Peroxidase Test,* of which there are several variants, the most widespread being the Kastel-Meyer Test. The suspect substance is removed and placed into a dish into which are added 130mg of phenolphthalein, 1.3gm of potassium hydroxide and 100ml of distilled water. The mixture is then boiled until it becomes clear. A further 20gm of powdered zinc is added while boiling. A few drops of hydrogen peroxide is then added. If the solution turns pink, the result is positive for the presence of blood.

Other methods of detecting blood involve the use of sprays, that either turn the stain a particular colour or cause it to fluoresce.

Luminol spray is used in dark conditions to detect blood. If it is present, fluorescence will occur. Another spray of phenolphthalein mixed with orthotolidine will result in a pink colour in the presence of blood.

DNA profiling today has extremely high discriminating power, and this has had the effect of focusing the attention of police scientists and the courts more frequently on questions concerning how blood-staining was caused. So <u>Bloodstain Pattern Analysis</u> (BPA) is now applied both at a crime scene and in the forensic laboratory to establish the distribution of blood. Blood pattern forensics has now become an essential and respected element of forensic science. DNA advances have revolutionised the way we look at blood and the information we can extract from it. It can literally identify the guilty and exonerate the innocent.

Chapter Seven: Trace And Contact Evidence

'Trace evidence' is the term applied to tiny amounts of material such as textile fibres, glass and paint, which can serve to link an item on which material is found, with an otherwise 'unconnected' source elsewhere. Finding such a trace implies that there has been direct 'physical contact' between the item and the source, resulting in the transfer of material between them.

The principle here is that attributed to Frenchman Edmund Locard. He was the first person to advance the theory that when someone commits a crime, they always leave something behind at the crime scene. They also always take away something which was not on them when they arrived, hence " *Every contact leaves a trace"*.

Textile fibres and paint are common forms of trace evidence in a large number of criminal cases. One of the main functions of the forensic scientist is to search through microscopic particles of material recovered from a crime scene, a victim, the suspect and elsewhere, and to recognise and distinguish between what appears to be 'in place' and what is 'out of place' at a particular scene.

This involves two different approaches, the most common being 'reactive' searching, whereby potentially useful sources of trace material are identified. These materials are searched for other items collected as a means of linking them together. In this way, the forensic scientist can focus attention on lines of enquiry which are considered most likely to yield significant findings. An alternative 'inceptive' approach is where items usually taken from a crime scene are searched for any trace materials which are distinctive and unrelated to them or the scene. These traces may point to a particular source and eventually lead to the offender.

[1] Glass

Glass possesses two beneficial properties concerning forensic science. It <u>refracts</u> light, and it has a specific <u>density</u>, both of which can be measured and used as a means of identifying fragments. This enables a conclusion to be made regarding the 'origin' of the glass. For example, did it come from the smashed window at the scene of a burglary? Or did it come from the bottle found broken at the scene of a murder? Often a suspect will have fragments of glass adhered to their clothes or shoes which can be compared with glass found at the crime scene. Forensic scientists have sophisticated apparatus including scanning electron microscopes which allow the determination of certain elements in samples to be made.

A somewhat less sophisticated procedure is initially used in the examination of glass. If it is coloured glass, two samples can be compared by eye. It is also possible to determine whether glass came from a 'flat' sheet or a 'curved' object like a bottle, by merely examining it. A slightly more complex procedure is the matching of pieces of glass together, which is possible if reasonably larger pieces are found. Glass fragments that appear as though they may fit together can be done by hand. Perfect fits will hold together very tightly, resisting separation.

It is not only the fragments themselves that hold useful information. It is the way a piece of glass 'broke' that can be used as evidence. For example, what happens when a bullet or a projectile travelling at <u>high speed</u> is shot through a window? The glass molecules at the <u>point of impact</u> will dislodge the molecules in front of it. This continues until the bullet emerges through the other side of the pane. The resulting hole will be <u>crater-shaped</u>, the larger end being the point of exit, the smaller, the point of entry. The presence of glass particles on the floor on the side where the bullet emerged will often reveal the direction of travel of the bullet. Conversely, a projectile travelling at 'low speed' hits the window, the 'crater-shaped' hole will not be formed. Instead, there will be a <u>star-like or radial</u> pattern of fractures emanating from the hole.

Circular or <u>arc-like fractures</u> are often seen around a hole connecting some of the radial fractures. These fractures will form on the <u>outside</u> of the window, the side struck by the projectile. It is difficult to distinguish between a hole made by a high-velocity bullet and one made by a pebble travelling at high speed. A window struck by a slow-moving stone will shatter in its entirety, as will one subjected to a close-range shot. However, the presence of gunpowder residues on the glass fragments will often indicate that a firearm was used. Sometimes, two or more bullets may pierce a window and, if radial fractures are present, it is possible to determine which shot was fired first. This is because the radial fractures caused by the <u>second</u> shot will end at the existing fractures caused by the first shot.

[2] Hair

Hairs found at a crime scene may belong to the offender, the victim or animals associated with either individual. Hairs provide useful evidence because they retain their structure for a long time. Unfortunately for investigators, there are often

101

significant variations in the structure of different hairs from a single individual, especially if they are from different parts of the same body. It is for this reason that the broadest possible range of comparison samples is taken for analysis. Under microscope technology, it is possible to tell whether a hair has been artificially bleached or coloured. Hair can also reveal the presence of poison in a body.

A hair that was forcibly removed from its owner will have a piece of scalp tissue adhering to its root. This can be used as a source of DNA fingerprinting. Even the hair itself contains mitochondrial DNA, which can be used to determine the maternal relationship.

[3] Textile Fibres

These are usually classified as being either 'natural, or 'synthetic', cotton being the most common, but today synthetic fibres are more widely used. Textiles are usually easier to identify than hairs, and there are reference collections and information available from manufacturers. Textile fibres are often dyed in various colours and woven in various patterns. Synthetic fibres contain certain chemicals which can be analysed and identified.

One of the underlying assumptions of forensic science is that a person, present at a crime scene exchanges 'trace' evidence with that location in several different ways. Traces may be found at the scene that can be linked to a suspect. Traces found on the suspect may then link him or her to that same crime scene. Hairs, fibres, paint, dust, soil, plant debris and paint flakes can all be examined. All fibres used in clothing and furnishings today are natural, synthetic or a combination of the two.

Natural fibres include wool and silk, cotton

and hemp. Each one has a characteristic appearance to enable it to be distinguished from human and other animal hairs. It is sometimes possible to identify fragments of fabric. For example, forensic scientists can sometimes match a length of fibre from the clothing of a hit-and-run victim with a fragment found on the vehicle responsible for the accident.

[4] Paint Evidence

Traces of paint evidence, particularly the colour of a flake of paint can be matched with the surface from which it was taken. In others, the chemical constituents and other properties of the sample can be determined to prove whether or not they match the suspected source. Paint samples are particularly important in cases involving vehicles. Forensic laboratories have access to large databases on the precise composition and ranges of colours used by paint manufacturers. The surface finish of any vehicle is usually built - up as a series of layers, from the initial 'primer' to the final coats of clear gloss. Colours can be compared under the microscope, and the polymer binder that holds each layer together can be broken down and analysed by gas chromatography. This helps to establish points of comparison with other samples taken from suspect surfaces.

In respect of trace material recovered from crime scenes, it is of considerable importance to ensure that any material could not have arisen because of accidental <u>contamination</u>, between one of them and another. Such contamination known as '<u>secondary transfer</u>', can occur if someone seizes, handles or comes into contact with items from more than one location. In such circumstances, traces may have been 'accidentally' transferred by that person's hand or clothes. Only routine procedures and protocols, designed to avoid contamination will ensure that there can be a high level of confidence about the integrity of items examined by forensic scientists.

Chapter Eight: Destruction By Fire

Fire investigation is one of the most difficult that is routinely carried out by the forensic scientist. It is a fact that the most significant loss of evidence at the scene of a fire occurs during the cleaning-up and salvage procedures. Evidence of directional heating effects, smoke records, temperature indications and implicative trace evidence may remain.

Identification of the cause, whether accidental or deliberate, is recognised as significant for the prevention of further fires and in bringing offenders to justice.

The three main requirements for a fire to occur are <u>heat</u>, <u>oxygen</u> and <u>fuel.</u> For a fire to start fuel must be heated in the presence of oxygen, to a temperature sufficient to initiate a chemical reaction. The most commonly used fuels contain <u>carbon,</u> <u>hydrogen</u> and <u>oxygen.</u> Once a reaction has been initiated, sufficient heat must be produced for the fire to continue.

Before examining how fire is forensically investigated, the scientists need to pose the question; "Why do some people deliberately set out on a course of fire-raising?" There is all manner of reasons, but the most common one is a desire to conceal another crime. However, it is very rare for fires to be started to commit murder. Similarly, 'suicide' is very rarely committed by fire, for the simple reason it will be too painful for the victim to endure. However, there have been rare occasions when some people have committed suicide in this way but mainly political protesters to draw public attention to their grievances.

More commonly, fire-raising or to give it the legal definition <u>Arson</u> is committed for <u>economic</u> reasons. A robber might burn down a building

105

containing 'stolen' goods, the intention being to create an impression that the fire would be seen as the cause of the disappearance of the goods and 'robbery' may not be suspected. The records or actual stock of a business may be destroyed by a dishonest employee to cover up fraudulent activities. Also, someone wishing to cheat an insurance company may fire his own property.

Malice and revenge are 'motives' for arson, but there are more complex motives. Fire itself, does appear to have a fascination for most people and some psychologists believe it arouses primaeval feelings in most people, but no real harm comes from them. However, it is when such feelings are developed to cause havoc deliberately, that such instinct leads to arson. In fact, the desire to destroy for actual gain is a more common reason for arson than most people can imagine. The first thing that needs to be established during a fire investigation is where the fire originated.

When a fire starts to burn in a building, the structural wooden beams will be subjected to high temperatures for a longer time than will woodwork in other parts of the building. Consequently, the extent of charring will be greater in the former than the latter. As a crucial general observation, the lowest point in which the results of intense burning can be seen, is probably the point of origin, since fire tends to spread upward.

The intensity of a fire's point of origin can also be gauged by the extent of damage to other components in the building. For example, glass will distort when subjected to temperatures above 700°C, while at temperatures above 850°C, it will flow and trickle. The steel beams used in modern buildings may also distort at high temperatures. It is sometimes possible to detect the direction in which the fire moved by examining particular objects that have suffered more considerable fire damage on one side of the building than the other. Also, plaster may break away from the brickwork when subjected to high temperatures, and this may indicate the intensity of the fire at particular places within the building. Also, smoke detectors may record the order in which they were activated and may be recovered to provide additional information.

There are small clues that can aid in reconstructing the events of the fire. For example, smoke blackening at the top of a door indicates that the door was open during the fire; otherwise blackening would have been observed over the whole surface of the door. Also, lines of severe burning on the ground surrounded by areas of less burning indicate that a trail of petrol was laid by the arsonist. A large mound of combustible material in one location may suggest a case of arson, together with signs of forced entry, e.g. doors forced, broken windows with glass fragments lying inside the building and broken locks - all of these point to deliberate fire-raising.

The search for faulty electrical equipment must also be a priority.

Apart from such things as signs of forced entry, what arouses suspicion in the mind of a fire investigator?

One obvious answer must be evidence that the fire was caused deliberately. This also raises another question, what constitutes such evidence?

It could be concluded that there was more than one origin of the fire. An accidental fire will have only one source because it would be highly unlikely that two accidental fires could start at the same time and in the same building. Consequently, when the evidence appears to show that the fire began in more than one location, this would justify a conclusion that the fire had been started deliberately, and therefore a case of Arson.

The Use of Accelerants

Arsonists usually use an accelerant to start a fire such as a flammable liquid like petrol which is poured over a wide area of carpets and furnishings. Then a match is applied. This ensures that a hot-fire will follow and the building will be well-alight before any fire-fighters arrive on the scene. However, a factor unknown to most arsonists is that traces of accelerants can be detected even after the building has been destroyed. This is because small amounts of accelerant will seep into carpets, floorboards, plaster and brickwork, and will not be consumed by the fire. In addition, the cooling effects of hosed water will slow down the rate of evaporation of the accelerant, leaving enough to be detected.

'Sniffing' devices which are hydrocarbon detectors are often used to test objects at the scene, to confirm whether they contain accelerants. An extended nozzle is attached via a cable to a box with a display monitor. The principle applied is almost that of a domestic 'vacuum cleaner'. The air around the object (often a piece of floor-board) is sucked into the nozzle and into the box, where it passes over a heated filament.

If an accelerant is detected, it will be oxidised and raise the temperature of the filament. This increase in temperature will be recorded as a deflection on the monitor. Such a device is typically used to indicate if a more detailed investigation is required.

Common accelerants used by arsonists include petrol, paraffin, methylated spirits, alcohol, turpentine, diesel and other flammable solvents. If an incendiary device has been used in the attack, the remains may still be found at the fire scene. The wick and shattered bottle of a *Molotov Cocktail* can often be found.

It is a known fact that people caught up in a fire often react in unpredictable ways. It may appear odd that they were unable to escape when the scene is examined, and the fire has been extinguished. Both visibility-impairing smoke and terror can make people rush towards the fire rather than away from it.

Also, the inhalation of *carbon monoxide* (CO) will reduce the ability of the victim to flee because the reduced amount of *haemoglobin* available for carrying oxygen, will result in muscular weakening, leading to collapse. With CO concentrations of around 20-30%, this will make the victim feel unwell with headaches and dizziness. 40% saturation will result in a lack of muscular coordination and mental confusion. At 50%, these effects become more pronounced when slurred speech, weakness and vomiting occur. By about 60%, the victim will lose consciousness, and with concentrations of 70% or above, death will follow rapidly.

Absence of CO from the blood in bodies recovered after a fire is very suspicious and indicates criminal activity. Anyone dying in a fire will have a certain amount of CO concentration in the blood.

Explosives

There are two kinds of explosive, low and high. Low explosives are characterised by their ability to burn like any other combustible material. They only become explosive when they are confined to a small space. The typical low explosives are <u>black powder</u> or gunpowder and smokeless powder. All low explosives are essentially mixtures of an oxidising agent and a fuel. 'Black-powder' is a mixture of <u>saltpetre</u> (potassium nitrate), charcoal and sulphur. It can be used as a fuse to ignite a larger amount of powder confined in a container. 'Smokeless powder' is made of *nitrocellulose* (cotton treated with nitric acid) or a mixture of *nitroglycerine and nitrocellulose*). It is a more powerful explosive than 'black-powder'. When a low explosive explodes, it exerts a <u>throwing effect,</u> in which objects are hurled about and walls blown apart. Mixtures of air and fuel explode with a similar effect, but some gas will remain unconsumed and, as air rushes back to the area of the explosion, oxygen will combine with the remaining hot gas, and fire will break out. Often, it is this <u>secondary</u> fire that causes most of the damage and not the initial explosion. It is the sudden generation and expansion of gases within a container that causes the explosion. These gases cause forces sufficient to make buildings collapse.

    <u>High explosives</u> are far more damaging, and explode at rates of between 1,000 and 8,500 metres per second, their effect being a 'shattering' one. These explosives are of two kinds, both of which are used in a high explosive system. The first group consists of heat, shock and friction-sensitive compounds, such as *mercury fulminate*. They detonate violently even in a confined space. Given their extreme sensitivity, they are not used in the main charge but used to initiate the explosion. They are basically, detonators and primers. Most modern detonators are set off by an electric current that passes through a wire filament that then ignites the fuse-head, this, in turn, ignites the primary charge. This then ignites the base-charge of secondary

explosive, causing the main explosive charge to detonate. This process can be best described as the classic 'Chain Reaction Principle'.

The main charge of high explosives usually a substance that burns rather than explodes, and is lit in small quantities in the presence of air. The most famous of these non-initiating explosives includes dynamite (nitroglycerine) mixed with an absorbent material, TNT (trinitrotoluene) and RDX (cyclotrimethylene trinitramine). When fragments of explosive are collected from a scene, the pieces are washed in acetone which dissolves most of the chemical components. Chromatography techniques are used to identify individual compounds. The result of the information on the composition of various explosives allows the forensic scientist to identify the particular make of the explosive used.

Forensic explosive investigators need to address many questions. "Was it an explosion?" "Was it an accident or a bomb?" "Was it a viable device or a hoax?" "Are there similarities that link the recovered items?" The source of forensic evidence usually found at the scene of the explosion will include power sources, timers, electronic, mechanical and chemical detonators, and mobile phones which can all be used as timing devices.

Since debris from a blast can be hurled considerable distances, the rule of thumb is for forensic teams to conduct their search in a circle around the blast point up to the point where the furthest fragment from the blast is located and then widen the radius of the search area by at least 20%. Meticulous records are essential, and the search for forensic evidence should be continued until the entire blast area has been covered.

The search methods will depend upon the

number of personnel available, the size and physical layout of the blast area, and the degree of destruction caused by the explosion. These searches are usually conducted using grid systems, spiral searches or line searches. Every piece of relevant material has to be catalogued and photographed *in situ*. It is also essential that the blast scene is recorded by both sketches and photographs, including aerial photography.

Contamination is a particular problem at blast sites, due to the large number of people and the variety of the agencies involved. Care must be taken to ensure that any evidence relating to explosives found at the scene is not handled or transported by any person or vehicles with previous recent exposure to explosives. This is to preserve the integrity and value of any exhibits presented as evidence in subsequent criminal trials.

Chapter Nine: Forensic Document Examination

The examination and analysis of documents is an important area of forensic science. All kinds of clues to the identity of a criminal can be revealed by fragments of writing, ranging from personal letters to ransom demands. Forged or altered letters, cheques, and other financial documents can be profitable for a criminal if they can be passed off as genuine. Forensic scientists use a wide range of techniques to reveal that documents are forgeries. Documents can be tested to help prove their authenticity, usually by analysis of the writing, and testing of the paper and ink, watermarks and most importantly, the signatures.

Handwriting Text

The identification of handwriting is one of the few forensic sciences that identifies the <u>individual</u>. It is a fact that handwriting can be identified. Most adults can recognise the handwriting of their immediate family and friends. Each person's handwriting displays a particular combination of character forms which gives that writing <u>individuality.</u> The basic shapes and construction of handwritings are taught in primary school, where children tend to learn their teachers' version of handwriting. The more 'individual' version of handwriting tends to begin during the teenage years when individuals begin to experiment with the appearance of handwriting. The handwriting of any individual tends to attain maturity during early adulthood and remains relatively constant in shape and proportion over the years, only changing as a result of old age.

Forms of Variation in Handwriting

Very few people write every character in the same manner on every single occasion. All handwriting will show some <u>natural</u> variation in the shape and proportions of characters. Consequently, sufficient handwriting samples must be available for examination to enable the range of <u>natural variation</u> to be determined. If insufficient handwritings are available for examination, there will always be the problem of not knowing if any differences have arisen because they were written by a 'different' person or as the result of natural variation in the handwriting of <u>one</u> person.

Handwriting experts study in detail how particular letters have been formed in any given sample. For example, the letter "i" may not be 'dotted', may be written without an upstroke or may have been written with one or more small 'eyelets', where the movement of the pen changed direction in forming the letter. Not only do these characters slow up throughout a particular sample of handwriting text, but in many cases, they are present even when the writer is trying to conceal identity or attempting to 'imitate' someone else's handwriting. Another area of analysis involves the <u>proportion</u> or relative <u>height</u> of different letters. Even in an individual's ordinary handwriting, variations do occur, but certain established <u>ratios</u> are usually <u>consistent</u>. For example, the ratio of the letter "g" above the line to the overall height of the letter will tend to remain the same in an individual writer, regardless of their writing <u>style</u>. Also, the overall <u>slant</u> of the writing from the 'vertical' is another reasonably consistent factor. This slant can range from $35°$ to the right and as much as $50°$ to the left. However, this should be more or less consistent for a given individual's hand.

Experts measure the inclination using a transparent protractor concentrating on the largest letters, e.g. "f", " h" or "g". Also, the spacing of individual letters, words or links, is another specific area in which writer's styles can differ. In particular, a signature or a complete line of text tends to follow a consistent path for an individual. The baseline is either straight, downward or both. The presence or absence of connectors, the strokes that join up letters in handwritten text, is another common individual variation. Handwriting can vary for several reasons; illness, increasing age, the influence of alcohol or drugs, stress and tiredness. However, these problems indicate a lack of pen-control and do not result in fundamental differences in structure.

Handwritings can also be disguised, but their inconsistencies often give them away. The 'slope' of a piece of handwriting may vary, or unusual character forms may appear. An attempt can be made to simulate another person's handwriting. However, any such attempt at simulation is a compromise between accuracy and fluency. To simulate another person's handwriting, a person must suppress their natural handwriting characteristics. This is technically a difficult process which cannot be maintained over long periods. As a result, the simulated handwriting will show characteristics of both the simulator and the target handwriting with the balance changing as time proceeds.

Handwritings undergo the most considerable degree of change in adolescence when the individual style is forming and old age when pen control becomes increasingly difficult. Mature handwriting can also undergo developmental changes over long periods. By using the 'variation', it is quite possible to place a piece of handwriting within a specific time-

<u>frame</u>.

Conclusions of Handwriting Examinations

Once the comparison of two handwriting samples is completed, the forensic document examiner will gather together observations of both the differences and the similarities in the structure, shape and proportions of the samples, to draw the appropriate conclusions. These are based not only on the number of similarities but also their quality. In all handwriting comparisons, the presence of differences is of vital significance. The presence of even a single, consistent difference between handwritings, must be explained because it is a reliable indicator of <u>different authorship.</u> However, where there is a sufficient quantity of both <u>questioned</u> and <u>genuine</u> comparisons, and they match in all respects without any significant differences being detected, then a firm conclusion as to <u>common authorship</u> can be given.

The Examination of Signatures

Signatures are very specialised pieces of handwriting, and there are specific problems involved in their identification. Our signature is the piece of handwriting which we all use most frequently. Because we use our signature so often, it becomes virtually <u>unconsciously</u> produced each time it is written.

The most significant problem in identifying signatures as genuine or forgeries is the small amount of comparable material which is contained within a signature.

In effect, signature identification is one of the most challenging areas of forensic document examination. The basis of signature identification is very similar to that of handwriting in general.

However, since signatures are used for personal identification, they are frequently the targets of forgery. Consequently, considerable effort will be made in attempts to <u>simulate</u> another person's signature. This can be achieved in many ways. If a document bearing a genuine signature is placed on a window or a sheet of glass over a light source and overlaid by another document, it is possible to <u>trace</u> the outline of the genuine signature on to the forged document. Such tracing is often made in <u>pencil</u> which can then be inked over. The resulting forgery although <u>superficially</u> similar to the genuine one, will be detectable by its lack of <u>fluency</u> as the forger follows the line of the original signature and by making mistakes in the detailed construction of the character formations.

Guide lines may be left on the document, and even if only fragments remain, these can be detected by viewing the signature under specialised lighting conditions. Also, guidelines may be in the form of 'indented' impressions on the target document. These are produced by placing a genuine signature on top of the target document. The 'genuine' signature is written over <u>heavily</u> so that impressions are transferred to the document underneath. These are then inked in to produce the simulation. These impressions can be easily detected by light shone at a shallow oblique angle to the document. Also, the signature is likely to lack fluency and contain mistakes similar to direct tracing.

<u>Simulated</u> signatures are not 'natural' writings. When producing a simulated signature, a forger must suppress their natural writing characteristics and adopt those of the person whose signature is the target, adopted. Although signatures made by one individual all differ slightly, certain

features in each example remain constant. For example, the placing of the signature relative to the typed or printed text in the letter. Other similarities are associated with the actual shape of the signature rather than the formation of individual letters. By placing a piece of tracing paper over a signature and marking the tops or bottoms of each of the letters, and then joining them all up, a zigzag line will be produced.

Genuine examples of the same signature all show a very similar line. A forgery (even one that seems on the surface to be quite convincing) often shows a different pattern from the original.

Other comparisons can be made by marking any gaps in the signature, which will also produce a characteristic pattern.

The baseline of a text of writing is another crucial element. Some forgers, concentrating on the formation of letters, fail to notice how the signature as a whole climbs and descends from left to right. Microscopic examination can show discrepancies between a genuine signature, usually written quickly and confidently, and a forgery, where the writer took care to make the shape as convincing as possible.

One way of confirming the identity of a writer is by locating the origin of the document under scrutiny. A search of a suspect's home or office may uncover partially destroyed drafts. Examination of the papers of a notepad may show pressure marks of a pen where a document was written. Modern forensic science techniques are employed, such as ESDA (*Electrostatic Detection Apparatus*) can highlight indentations on paper. This technique makes use of a physical phenomena that is not understood scientifically. When a piece of paper is indented, its properties change. ESDA releases an electrostatic charge through the paper which is kept at an angle. A mixture of photocopy toner and small glass beads is sprinkled over the paper. The altered electrical properties in the indented areas of the paper attract the toner-covered beads, making the indentation legible.

The Examination of Paper

The size, thickness, density, colour and finish of paper can be compared to determine if they are from a similar or different origin. Optical brighteners are incorporated into some papers and give different reactions when viewed in ultraviolet light. The organic fibres used in a particular paper manufacture can be identified by microscopy and used to give a broad geographical origin of the paper.

The origin of a paper is most accurately identified by its watermark. Some paper manufacturers periodically introduce changes into watermarks. However, not all manufacturers keep detailed records of these changes made over the years. This is usually due to company take-overs and absorption of some of the older brands.

The requirement for adequate comparable material in signature examination is similar to that required in all handwriting comparisons. However, it is important to stress that 'like' can only be compared to 'like'. Therefore, signatures are only comparable with other signatures in the same name. The ideal comparison material is one of genuine signatures close in time to the date of the signature under investigation. Given a reasonably stable and mature signature, and an adequate range of genuine signatures for comparison, the forensic examiner can expect to identify a genuine signature or a simulation. However, there will undoubtedly be occasions where only a 'qualified' conclusion can be given. This is because handwriting is, to an extent, a voluntary act and can be consciously changed. This being the case, it is unusual to be able to say with total confidence, that a person was not the author of a particular piece of handwriting.

In general, forensic document examiners use a five-point scale in their calculations about the possibility of whether a particular individual was the author of a specific document or not:

1. Common Authorship - 100% positive written by same person.
2. Highly Probable - Strong positive evidence written by same person.
3. Probable - Could very well have been written by same person.
4. Inconclusive - Insufficient evidence either way.
5. No evidence - No evidence to support the view that suspect was the author.

The identification of forgeries is one of the oldest of the forensic sciences going back to Roman times. The examination of documents in modern forensic science laboratories is an up-to-date science exploiting modern technology to cope with the ever-increasing demands made by sophisticated documentation. Forensic document examiners can demonstrate a solid scientific base for their particular areas of expertise.

Chapter Ten: The Presentation Of Forensic Evidence In Court

The outcome of most criminal investigations in the United Kingdom will be a trial. Similarly, the conclusion of every forensic science investigation will be the publication of a scientific report. This will provide the results and of the scientific tests performed, and will present these in a form that is accessible to all those involved.

In addition, there are occasions when a particular forensic scientist is required to appear in court, to explain and defend the conclusions they have reached in the final report.

The United Kingdom, as in the USA and other Commonwealth countries, uses an <u>adversarial</u> system of trials. According to the UK common law tradition, witnesses are called by both the prosecution and defence to answer questions. They are then subjected to cross-examination by the other party. The role of the judge is to make decisions on points of law. In an adversarial system, the <u>expert</u> witnesses are called to provide evidence to strengthen the case of the party that called them.

The responsibility for prosecuting cases in England and Wales lies with the Crown Prosecution Service (CPS). Based on a *realistic prospect of conviction,* CPS solicitors and barristers will present their cases in court.

The vast majority of criminal cases are tried at Magistrates' Court. Magistrates only commit the most serious and complex cases to the Crown Court. It is here that the defendant is tried before a judge and jury, and the full range of sentences available may be used for a defendant found guilty. Because of the serious nature of the offences, it is usual for a forensic scientist to be called to provide evidence at Crown Court rather than at Magistrates' Court.

The role of witnesses in criminal trials is to provide the court with information that is directly relevant to the particular case being heard. For the majority of these witnesses, their evidence will be limited to those facts directly relevant to the case.

Forensic scientists possess specialist expertise. They use this to interpret the scientific test results and relate these interpretations to the judge, jury and general court. There are circumstances with results of certain DNA profiling tests, where the evidence may appear so powerful that the forensic scientist may believe that it is 'beyond any reasonable doubt' that another individual might be responsible for the crime. However, the expert must guard against making such claims. The question of a defendant's guilt or innocence does not fall within the remit of the expert, nor any other witness.

This question is one that must ultimately be addressed by those responsible for deciding the case, namely the magistrates or the jury. The responsibility of the prosecuting lawyer, either solicitor or barrister, is to present the case against the defendant. They must collect and present to the court such facts as will show that the accused committed the crime with which they are charge *'beyond any reasonable doubt'*. Likewise, the responsibility of the defence lawyer is to counter the arguments put forward by the prosecution and to demonstrate that the prosecution has not made a convincing case. Though witnesses on both sides are presenting evidence of <u>fact</u>, it is also likely that they will have a personal view as to the guilt or otherwise of the defendant. In this sense, both sides are <u>partial</u> and <u>biased</u> to the party they represent.

It is a cardinal rule that any expert witness must stand apart from this partiality. The role of the expert witness is to use his or her experience and skill to provide 'impartial' and' unbiased' evidence in court. The overriding responsibility of the forensic scientist is to search for verifiable scientific facts and to provide such impartial evidence to the court. This does raise a legitimate question as to why it is necessary for both the prosecution and defence to employ their own experts. A basic tenet of the criminal justice system as practised in the UK is to ensure what is termed as *'equality of arms'.*

Equality of arms ensures the maximum probability of a fair trial, as whatever facility is made available to one side, should also be made available to the other. So if the prosecution intends to rely on scientific findings as part of their evidence at trial, it is only fair that the defence should be able to 'independently' test the strength of that evidence.

However, it would be very rare for experts to disagree over the scientific facts adduced in any particular case. Where such differences do arise, it is most likely to be with the interpretation placed on the findings. A particular area of difficulty in the interpretation of expert evidence by the courts is in the communication of risk and probability. The courts ultimately have to make a clear judgement about the case, and scientists can rarely give black and white answers.

Instead, they have to present a range of possibilities with, as far as possible, some indication of their relative probabilities.

A common pitfall in the treatment of DNA evidence has been the so-called prosecutor's fallacy. It arises when the prosecution equates a statistical probability with the likelihood of guilt based on a

123

statistical probability, For example, if the frequency of a particular DNA profile is one in a billion, and there is a match between the DNA profile of the suspect and the DNA profile of a forensic sample from the crime scene, one way of presenting this would be *"The chance of obtaining this DNA profile of the DNA in the crime sample from an individual other than the suspect is one in a billion"*. However, this is sometimes inaccurately presented. Consequently, there is too much potential for misinterpretation by a jury.

There is still a great deal of confusion regarding the best approaches for the presentation of statistical evidence to juries, even for DNA evidence which has now become a routine part of many criminal investigations. In some areas of science, there is room for genuine ambiguity about the meaning of particular scientific findings. For example, certain post-mortem findings in the view of one forensic pathologist may point to one conclusion about the origin of particular injuries. In contrast, another pathologist may consider a different conclusion. It is often not possible to determine that one expert is more 'correct' than the other. In such cases, the court will be left to decide between the two experts.

The Forensic Scientist's Report

The Report is the product of all the work which has been undertaken into the investigation. It must contain all relevant detail and be presented in a format that is accessible to the non-scientist or jury member. In the majority of cases in which the forensic scientist does appear in court to give expert evidence, the Report must be <u>concise</u> without the need for explanation or clarification by its author. It is

124

also vital that the Report is clear and unambiguous and contains all the necessary information to explain the scientific findings. While there is no standard template for the format of the Report, it should usually contain the following information. The relevant personal details of the scientist who compiled the Report including name, laboratory and relevant qualifications would be included. The central part of the report would be an outline of the particular crime. It would include a chronological sequence of the course of events of the incident under investigation. It should also include sufficient detail of the scientific tests and examinations which have been carried out.

This outline should indicate the expert examination's scope and depth and indicate the questions that the examination has addressed, together with those that cannot be addressed. It is usual practice to list all the items or exhibits examined, and to note from whom the items have been obtained, to maintain the *'chain of continuity'*.

This chain proves that proper tracking has been demonstrated regarding the progress of every item - from the moment of recovery at the crime scene to the time it is produced in court.

The work undertaken by the forensic scientist should describe the examination and test procedure carried out on the various items of evidence. The scientists should also explain the justification for each procedure carried out and provide a comprehensive summary of the results obtained.

Every procedure must be placed in context so that readers are aware of the overall rationale, and of the meaning and limitations of the results obtained. The results of every procedure carried out need to be interpreted within the context of the individual case.

There will be occasions on which the information adduced from the scientific tests appear to be of more value to the 'other side', either the prosecution or defence.

For example, a forensic scientist briefed by the prosecution may find that the results of specific tests carried out may assist the defence. Alternatively, a defence scientist may turn up information of value to the prosecution. In such a scenario, the forensic scientist has a duty not to withhold such information from the other side. The results of the various test should be drawn together to form a series of conclusions. This should be clear and unambiguous.

Disclosure of Expert Evidence

The forensic scientist working for the police must ensure that officers are made aware of all the scientific evidence relevant to the case, which must also be passed on to the CPS. In turn, this information will be disclosed to the defence. They must also be informed of anything on which the prosecution's scientist may have relied in forming the scientific conclusions. Following such disclose, the defence is entitled to access to case files and any other information used by the prosecution's scientists. There is a duty upon this scientist to retain pertinent documents and materials so that they may be made available to the defence if required. *Under the Crown Court (Advance Notice of Expert Evidence) Rules 1987*, the defence must disclose to the prosecution any expert evidence on which it may wish to rely at trial.

The duties of a forensic scientist are to examine material collected or submitted to provide information previously unknown, or on information already available. The scientist must provide the results of any examination in a Report that will enable the investigators to identify an offender or corroborate other evidence to facilitate the preparation of a case for prosecution in court. Finally, the scientist must present written or verbal evidence to a court to enable it to reach an appropriate decision as to guilt or innocence. The scientist must be able to demonstrate competence, impartiality and integrity. To facilitate these, the scientist should only give evidence of work carried out personally or under their direct supervision. Where scientific examination is relied on for legal purposes, the methods used should be based on 'established scientific principles', validated and published in reputable scientific literature. The presentation of evidence in both written and oral form is the culmination of the work undertaken by the forensic scientist in fulfilling their investigation.

Consequently, the scientist must ensure that their evidence is accurate, reliable and presented in a manner that it can be clearly and easily understood by those who require access to the information.

"The job of forensic science is to support the legal system from the crime scene to the courtroom. But everything depends on that final stage being scrupulous and even-handed. That is not only in the best interest of science, it's in the best interests of all of us."
Source: *"Forensics: The Anatomy of Crime"*, Val Mc Dermid, (Profile Books Ltd, London, 2015) p.289.

Chapter Eleven: The DNA Database Debate

Biometrics and Biometric Databases

Biometrics is defined as the identification of people by their personal traits or characteristics. There are two types of biometric identifiers. The first concerns the physiological characteristics, e.g. fingerprints, DNA, facial recognition and retina recognition. The second type concerns the behavioural identifiers, which include a person's 'walk' or gait and their voice. There are different considerations about how useful particular personal traits will be as biometric identifiers. One important consideration is whether the trait is universal. For example, every person in every society has fingerprints and DNA.

Consequently, this is why they are considered a good source of biometric information. The other consideration is whether this particular trait is permanent, in that it does not change in individuals over time. Hence, traits like fingerprints and DNA are stable throughout one's lifetime. It is also important that good sources of biometric information cannot be imitated or substituted by other people. It is hardly surprising that DNA and fingerprints are so useful in criminal investigations. They both have the potential to be easily recovered from crime scenes and samples taken from suspects for comparison.

The first fingerprint cataloguing system was introduced in Argentina in 1891, while the first national DNA database was established in the UK in 1995. In both cases, these types of databases have proven to be very valuable tools during criminal investigations. However, they also raise significant privacy and human rights issues which have proved to be controversial.

DNA profiling was discovered in 1984 at the University of Leicester in the UK, by Professor Sir Alec Jeffreys. The first criminal case in England was solved by using DNA in 1985-6. Then in 1987, the first UK DNA laboratory was established at the Forensic Science Service, the national government-funded forensic science provider in the UK.

The reason why it took over a decade between the development of DNA properly and the National DNA Database was because technological and legislative advances had to be established. Technological advances included the capacity to allow DNA profiles to be loaded, stored and searched electronically.

Running parallel to this was the requirement for legislative changes. In 1995 when the database was being established, there was no legislation to allow police to take DNA from suspects, retain and search them on a national database. As a result, changes had to be made to the *Police and Criminal Evidence Act 1984* to allow that to happen. The position in 1995 when the DNA database was established, the legislation at that time allowed the police to take DNA samples only from persons who had been convicted of criminal offences. In reality, this meant that a suspect had to be arrested, charged and convicted to have their DNA legally taken, retained indefinitely and searched against other crime scene DNA profiles.

In 2001, the legislation changed to allow the police to take DNA from anyone charged with a criminal offence. So a person no longer had to be found guilty or convicted; they just needed to be charged by the police. Their DNA was taken and loaded onto the DNA database and searched against existing crime scene profiles. Once again, in 2004, another change relaxed the requirements, this time to allow police to take DNA profiles from anyone who was <u>arrested</u> for any recordable offence.

The consequence of this was that suspects did not need to be charged or convicted - but only arrested. When this happens, they are required to provide a DNA sample, together with their fingerprints and photograph. As a result of these legislative changes, there were noticeable statistical changes. In 2001, there were 1.5 million profiles loaded onto the National DNA Database. Then in March 2005, this increased to 3 million profiles. Within four years, the size of the Database had doubled, and by September 2012, there were approximately 6.6 million profiles. This number represented around 10% of the total population of the UK.

The National DNA Database and Police Investigations

The Database helps police investigations by providing the opportunity to link crimes which are believed to have been committed by the same offender. This can be done by linking <u>physical evidence</u> recovered from crime scenes to <u>one person</u>.

Whenever DNA is recovered from a crime scene, it is loaded onto the database and searched against all the profiles held. This search provides the police with an opportunity to confirm that the same DNA links a series of crimes.

The Database can also help police investigations through what is termed *<u>Speculative Searches</u>*. These are carried out when the police have no idea whose DNA they have recovered. It is loaded onto the Database in the hope that a 'hit' will be found with someone's profile held there. In the original legislation in 1995, 'speculative searches' were forbidden to form the basis for an arrest or prosecution. They could only be used as 'police intelligence', but not as evidence, but today, this practice is now allowed.

Another way that the Database can be used is a more modern approach referred to as <u>Familial Searching</u>. This allows police to load a crime scene sample onto the DNA database, and request the database to provide <u>close matches</u>. These are matches that are close enough to the crime scene DNA to indicate they may belong to individuals who are 'related' to the crime scene's DNA donor. The value of such a technique is that it provides investigative opportunities for the police to follow fresh leads.

Case Study

In September 2005, Sally Anne Bowman, an 18-year-old was murdered in South London. This murder resulted in an enormous scale investigation, including approximately 1,700 <u>voluntary</u> DNA samples from members of the public. None of these samples produced any valuable leads.

In June 2006, Mark Dixie was arrested for a relatively minor incident that occurred in a local pub. Dixie was required to provide a DNA sample as well as fingerprints and photograph. When the sample was loaded onto the National DNA Database, it produced a match with DNA samples taken from the Sally Bowman crime scene.

This is an excellent example of a case where the police had not previously identified Dixie as a suspect. As a result of a completely unrelated arrest, the police were able to solve a serious crime.

However, in recent years some of the concerns around the National DNA Database have focussed on human rights implications.

This concern was highlighted by two cases referred to as the *S and Marper* cases. The letter 'S' was used for the first defendant because he was a juvenile at the time of the criminal trial. These two individuals were not convicted of the crimes for which they had been arrested. They argued on appeal that their DNA and fingerprints should not be allowed to be retained by the police on the basis that they were found not guilty of the crimes for which they were arrested. In both cases, the Appeal Court agreed that the DNA and fingerprints should be allowed to be held indefinitely, even though neither man was eventually convicted of the crimes they were accused of committing. Both defendants took their cases to the European Court of Human Rights, arguing that this was a violation of their right to 'a private life', and of their 'right to keep their private information private' The ruling at the European Court was unanimously in favour of the two defendants.

The Court maintained that keeping the information, which in this case was the DNA and fingerprints, could not be regarded as necessary in a 'democratic' society. Therefore, the UK's retention policy of keeping peoples' DNA and fingerprints indefinitely, regardless of the outcome of the trial, was in breach of the European Human Rights Charter. As a result, the UK Government was forced to implement new legislation, and in October 2013, the *Protection of Freedoms Act* was implemented. This Act highlighted the importance of the outcome of the trial, and also the age of the offender, the seriousness of the offence and the outcome of the investigation. This does not change the fact that the police can still take DNA and fingerprints on arrest. However, it does affect how long and in which circumstances they can hold that information indefinitely.

To summarise, DNA is still taken on arrest, so that has not changed since the 2013 Act. The police can take DNA upon arrest regardless, but the first question which needs answering is whether or not the person was subsequently charged with the crime for which they were arrested.

If the answer is no, this questioner must ask if they were arrested for a relatively minor offence or a serious one.

If it was a minor offence and they were found innocent of it, their DNA can be retained for up to three years before being removed.

If the person is arrested, charged and convicted, the question then becomes, how old is the offender? If they are under 18, they are classed as a juvenile, and if it is a relatively minor offence, the DNA is retained for five years then removed.

However, if the offender is an adult and they are convicted of a crime, DNA is still retained indefinitely under the 2013 Act. So, the only way someone's DNA is now held indefinitely on the database is if they are arrested, charged and convicted of a criminal offence.

There is no question that DNA evidence has an excellent opportunity to contribute to police investigations and lead to the identification of those guilty. However, the implementation of the National DNA Database has resulted in some very complex ethical and privacy issues. The real question that the reader needs to ask at this point is, "What is the right balance between maintaining public safety through effective use of DNA databases, and the privacy that everyone is entitled to under human rights legislation?

Even though the relatively new *Protection of Freedoms Act* placed a lot of limitations on the indefinite retaining of DNA, there are still many who argue that we need to be 'expanding' our national DNA database rather than reducing or limiting it.

Consequently, there are some significant arguments in support of expansion. The first of these arguments is that <u>everyone</u> in society should be placed on the database. Then if a crime was committed, and DNA was available at the crime scene, then that DNA database has the potential to be 100% effective. It would follow that any crime-scene DNA recovered would potentially 'hit' or match someone on that database.

On these grounds, it would appear to be a significant advantage and therefore, a good reason for having a mandatory nation-wide database. Another argument put forward is the fact that currently, there is a stigma or *labelling effect* of being on the national DNA database. This is because it is a <u>police database</u> that holds DNA profiles and samples associated with criminal activity. The stigma is that you are a criminal or have been associated with a criminal act. Those arguing for 'expanding' the database are at pains to point out that this very stigma and labelling effect would disappear if everyone were required to be on the database. It would, in effect, no longer be a criminal database, but a nation-wide mandatory database.

Understandably, some strong arguments go against expanding the database. The first of these relates to the <u>cost-effectiveness</u> of a DNA database. By expanding the database to include everyone in the UK, this would require a massive investment of resources. Also, it would prove very difficult to enforce the required DNA samples for every member of the public. Another argument against the DNA database is that even if everyone were on it, it would produce a minimal increase in effectiveness. The reason put forward for this is because the vast majority of crime scenes which are part of all the recorded crime in England and Wales, do not have a DNA sample associated with them.

Consequently, the DNA database is only helpful in cases where there is a crime scene DNA profile, to be compared with people who are actually on that database. A final argument is that by increasing the size of the DNA database by including everybody, the chances of false matches would increase accordingly.

Although DNA is often perceived as 'infallible', there is always a small probability that any DNA so-called 'match' is a false-match.

Also, you can have 'supposed' matches between a suspect profile and crime-scene profile. There is always a small chance that the suspect did not leave the DNA at the crime scene, and it was, in fact, somebody else. As a result, we increase the risk of these false matches occurring because the increased number of people on the database would produce potential false-matches. In addition to privacy issues, another vital aspect to consider is the cost-effectiveness of the database.

It is vital to consider some basic statistics. The National DNA Database actually assists police in less than 50% of all recorded crime in England and Wales. Also, the database costs approximately 7% of annual police budgets. However, it is also important to consider that the crimes that the database does assist are more likely to be the most serious crimes that police investigate. It is difficult to put a price on being able to solve these types of crime sooner than would otherwise be the case due to the use of the database.

There are, of course, other issues to consider in addition to cost-effectiveness and human rights. One other thing to consider in terms of the effectiveness of the database is the fact that it is widely believed that violent crime is mainly perpetrated by people who are known to the <u>victim.</u>

In such cases, DNA is quite often not useful because it is not a question for the police of who did it, but what happened? So DNA is not particularly useful in crimes like domestic-violence related, where the perpetrator's identity is relatively clear. Also, it needs to be kept in mind that 'most' crime scenes do not yield <u>biological</u> evidence that will provide a DNA profile.

In this chapter, we have considered several arguments regarding the 'expansion' of the National DNA Database, and have looked at arguments both in favour and against the proposal. It is a sensitive and challenging issue to debate. It requires consideration of the most appropriate <u>balance</u> between public safety and the law enforcement and crime-fighting potential of DNA, and an individual's right to protection of private and personal information.

Chapter Twelve: The Future Of Forensic Science

The United Kingdom's Forensic Science Service (FSS), a government-owned agency, provided forensic services to the police and government agencies in England and Wales, together with overseas clients. However, in March 2012, the FSS was closed down over claims that it was losing between 1 and 2 million pounds a month, and that there was a 'shrinking' in the forensic market in the UK.

The role of the FSS was taken up by a combination of private forensic providers (PFPs) and police 'in-house' laboratories sharing the work. In July 2013, the UK Government Science and Technology Committee reported on an Inquiry conducted into the state of forensic science in the UK.

The Committee found that many of the 43 police forces in England and Wales were undertaking what they termed 'low- level' evidence processing, and screening 'in- house'. This was considered to be a result of the austerity measures imposed on the police service by the then government. The police 'rationale' was to save money from their annual budgets and undertake some 'low-level' forensic work themselves, thus avoiding having to send samples to private forensic providers.

In 2008, the UK Home Office established a new position of Forensic Science Regulator to set up, monitor and maintain <u>quality</u> standards in the provision of forensic science. What the Committee discovered was that many of the police forces were struggling to meet the <u>accreditation</u> requirements of the Forensic Science Regulator. The main concern for

137

the Committee was that there was 'fragmentation' in the forensic examination process between the police and the private providers. The consensus was that the situation might very well increase the possibility of vital pieces of forensic evidence being missed, or links between different items of evidence not being realised.

However, by 2017, all aspects of forensic science in the UK operated to one single quality standard framework based on the Regulator's Codes of Practice and Conduct. These Codes are compliant with the International Organisation for Standardisation Standard 17025 or ISO 17025. In the forensic context, this standard specifies the requirements for managing forensic scene services laboratories, and to demonstrate consistency between products and services. In addition to laboratory accreditation, these Codes also cover crime scene examination, and how exhibits are recovered, transported and stored.

How Forensic Science Operates Today

The first stage of any forensic investigation is the collection of evidence which is usually undertaken by a civilian member of the police, a Scenes of Crime Officer or 'SOCO'. The second or analysis stage of investigation is carried out by a technician, whose main objective is to analyse evidence and produce relevant data.

The final stage of interpretation of the evidence is the responsibility of what we traditionally think of as a 'forensic scientist'. Their specific role is to interpret the evidential value of the technician's data. These are the people who would attend court to give evidence and to help the jury to understand what the forensic evidence indicates. While in the first stage, the SOCO would be very much part of the police team in the investigation, the analysis and interpretation stages would be undertaken by either private or government forensic laboratories. In the UK today, private laboratories undertake the bulk of forensic analysis for the police and the defence if required.

Most resources of the police, forensic laboratories and funds from central government are put into the identification evidence types of DNA and fingerprints. The reason for this particular emphasis is because both DNA and fingerprints have the ability, not only to provide evidence but also identify a suspect. Also, DNA and fingerprints are found at a variety of crime scenes, particularly those that constitute volume crimes, such as burglary and vehicle crimes.

These two types can provide the best form of evidence to give the police a 'realistic' chance of being able to solve a crime through forensic evidence. However, there are problems concerning the recovery of DNA evidence.

Cellular or contact DNA is quite often found at a crime scene, on weapons, tools, door handles and items of clothing. The main difficulty with this type of DNA is that it is virtually unseen, so you have to search for it speculatively.

Another problem is that as well as having the DNA on an item linked to an offender, it could also contain other people's DNA. Consequently, you would not just get the offender's DNA but everyone's DNA as a mixture. It is complicated to interpret such mixtures of DNA and to separate the individuals when there are more than two mixtures present on an item. These other mixtures of DNA might be from people who have no connection to the crime scene.

They would largely be unknown to the police and tough to identify.

In such situations, success with DNA in terms of being able to obtain a profile that is suitable for loading onto the database would be, at best, variable. The more visible items such as blood and saliva are more successful, while other things like food, where bacteria will rapidly degrade DNA, make it very difficult to get a single profile that is likely to be that of the offender.

With DNA sampling, another essential issue is that of contamination by SOCOs who collect it, or the technician or forensic scientists who analyse and interpret it. Another critical issue is that of innocent cross-contamination. For example, I might shake hands with someone and then touch a door handle, innocently transferring both my own and the other person's DNA onto the door handle.

Consequently, while their DNA is now on the door handle, this does not imply that at some point they actually touched the door handle. This is, in essence, cross-contamination. So these invisible DNA stains which may be cellular or contact, are much more difficult to interpret than are such visible stains as blood or bodily fluids.

A final issue is the need for preservation, of the DNA samples. It is essential to ensure that DNA evidence maintains integrity and continuity.

Fingerprints are one of the most common types of evidence to be found at crime scenes. These prints can either be recovered 'in situ' by the process of 'lifting' or can be removed for enhancement in a police crime laboratory.

What are the most recent developments in fingerprint technology?

In the early 1990s, the UK introduced its first

computerised storage and searching system for fingerprints known as *Automated Fingerprint Recognition* or AFR. However, this was not considered to be a true 'national' system, since all of the 43 England and Wales police forces did not employ it. This came in 2001 with a government-sponsored UK national computer system, the *National Automated Fingerprint Identification System* or NAFIS.

Around the same time, the UK police service and the government removed the '16-point Standard' for fingerprints. From then onwards, it became a matter of 'assertion' for an individual fingerprint expert to state whether they felt that two fingerprints were 'identical', based on their own experience and expertise.

In 2006, the *next generation* of national computer systems was introduced to replace the existing NAFIS. This was known as 'IDENT 1' which had many advances, including the storage and searching of both 'palms' and 'fingertips'. This system also included 'LIVESCAN' which enables electronic capture of fingerprints, removing the outdated need for ink and paper.

'Livescan' can also improve the quality of the stored fingerprints. This system also included Scotland, so it is very much a United Kingdom system. More recently, there has been the introduction of a 'Mobile I.D. System' which allows wireless identification of fingerprints. These can be carried out at a crime scene or the roadside by traffic police officers. This is part of the UK *'Information Systems Improvement Strategy'* or ISIS.

With regard to DNA advancements, we have seen that in 1995, the National DNA Database was set up with a profiling technique known as SGM (*Second*

Generation Multiplex). This is capable of sampling six different 'loci' along the DNA molecule, which can provide a 'discriminating power' of 1 in 50 million. In 1999, this was improved to SGM+, which enables more 'degraded' samples to be processed. It was around 2000 that there were incremental improvements in the variety of DNA techniques available to the police in the UK. One of these, *'Familial DNA'*, has been particularly popular and useful. If you have a DNA profile recovered from a crime scene for which there is no individual match on the database, 'familial' DNA allows a search to be done on the database for people with similar profiles to that obtained from the crime scene. The basic premise for 'familial DNA' is that you are very likely to have similar DNA to your close relatives, e.g. father, mother and siblings. So if you are not yourself on the DNA database as an offender, they may be.

In July 2014, 'DNA 17' was introduced into the UK. This can sample the 10 SGM+ 'loci' and another six, giving a statistical odds of 1 in a billion. Essentially, it provides improved sensitivity. This means that less or poor quality DNA that has become degraded or contaminated can now still provide a DNA profile. However, there are still several issues with 'DNA 17'; in particular, the risk of 'contamination'.

Because of the increased sensitivity, sample handling by the SOCOs or scientists needs to be very closely monitored.

What next for DNA profiling?

When a DNA profile is obtained from a sample recovered from a crime scene, if it does not match anyone on the DNA database, it is possible to indicate the sex and ethnicity of the person leaving the DNA. As the size of the DNA database is increased particularly with ethnic minorities, then indications will be given to the police for intelligence purposes; of likely hair colour, eye colour or any distinguishing facial features that might be on the person who left the DNA.

With DNA, there are specific profiling processes that have to be carried out, including DNA isolation, quantification and amplification. All of these processes tend to slow down the time taken to analyse a particular sample. Developments are being introduced into making these processes quicker and reducing the time from crime scene DNA recovery to searching the National DNA Database. Two areas are being considered. The first is to see if it is possible to profile the DNA from the crime scene without actually having to extract it.

Currently, a bloodstain found at a scene is recovered by 'swabbing' it before profiling. A possible route of rapid processing would be to profile it straight from the stain.

However, this begs the question, would it be possible to use technology at a crime scene to get the DNA directly onto the database?

In fact, such technology already exists to profile DNA at a crime scene. It is referred to as *'lab on a chip'* technology. Portable mobile equipment can be used at a crime scene to take a sample recovered and complete the process of obtaining a profile by wireless technology.

This raises a further question.

Would improving the accuracy and reducing the processing time for DNA warrant the storing of an individual's DNA on some large 'international' database?

In the UK, there have been moves towards having a unified national biometrics database, rather

143

than separate databases for DNA, photographs and fingerprints, which are currently stored on separate databases. Could all this not be combined into one large biometrics database? So on this hypothetical biometrics database, how long would it be before the government of the day, decides it would make more sense to add to it, such things as employment details, national insurance numbers and driving licence details?. Why stop at this, you might as well add health records and passport details. When all this information is sitting there in one central database, how long will it be before your biometrics database becomes a <u>BIG BROTHER</u> one?

Selected Bibliography

Black, S & Ferguson, E. (Eds). *Forensic Anthropology: 2000-2010*. (London, Taylor & Francis, 2011).

Canter, D. *Forensic Psychology: A Very Short Introduction*, (Oxford U.P. Oxford, 2010).

Cooke, R.A. & Ide, R.H. *Principles of Fire Investigation*, (Institute of Fire Engineers, Leicester, 1992).

Ellen, D.M. *The Scientific Examination of Documents*, (Ellis Horwood, Chichester, 1989).

Erzinclioglu, Z. *Maggots, Murder and Men,* (Harley Books, Colchester, 2000).

Ferner, R. E. *Forensic Pharmacology: Medicines, Mayhem and Malpractice,* (Oxford Medical Publications, 1996).

Frank, P. & Offoboni, A.*"The Dose Makes the Poison": A Plain Language Guide to Toxicology,* (Wiley-Blackwell, Oxford, 2011).

Fraser, J. *Forensic Science: A Very Short Introduction,* (Oxford University Press, 2010).

Garrett, G & Nott, A. *Causes of Death,* (Constable & Robinson, London, 2001).

Glaister, J. *Medical Jurisprudence and Toxicology,* (Livingstone, Edinburgh, Various Editions).

Gough, T.A. *The Analysis of Drugs of Abuse,* (John Wiley, Chichester, 1991).

Harvey, W. *Dental Identification and Forensic Odontology,* (Kimpton, London, 1976).

145

Kind, S. *Scientific Investigation of Crime*, (Forensic Science Service, Harrogate, 1987).

Knight, B. *Simpson's Forensic Medicine*, (Edward Arnold, London, 1991).

Lane, B. *Encyclopedia of Forensic Science*, (Headline, London, 1992).

Mc Dermid, V. *Forensics:* The *Anatomy of Crime,* (Profile Books, London, 2015).

Marriner, B. *Forensic Clues to Murder,* (Arnold Books, London, 1991).

Mason, J.K.*The Pathology of Violent Injury,* (Edward Arnold, London, 1978).

Paul, P. *Murder Under the Microscope,* (Macdonald, London, 1990).

Prag, J & Neave, R. *Making Faces*, (British Museum Publications, 1997).

Redmayne, M. *Expert Evidence and Criminal Justice,* (Oxford University Press, 2007).

Robertson, B. & Vignaux, G.A.*'Interpreting Evidence': Evaluating Forensic Evidence in the Court Room,* (Wiley, Chichester, 1995).

Robertson, J. *Forensic Examination of Fibres,* (Ellis Horwood, Chichester, 1999).

Simpson, K. *Forty Years of Murder,* (Granada Publishing, London, 1981).

Smith, S. *Mostly Murder*, (Harrap, London, 1986).

Stern, C. *Dr Iain West's Casebook*, (Little Brown, London, 1996).

Stockdale, R.E. (Ed), *Science Against Crime*, (Marshall Cavendish, London, 1982).

Timbrell, J. A. *Introduction to Toxicology*, (Taylor & Francis, London, 1968).

Walls, H.J. *Forensic Science,* (Sweet & Maxwell, London, 1968).

White, P.C. (Ed), *Crime Scene to Court: Essentials of Forensic Science,* (Society of Chemistry, Cambridge, 1998).

Printed in Great Britain
by Amazon